The Man You Could Be

paul w. downey

REFLECTIONS for teens

journeyforth®

Greenville, South Carolina

Cover Photo: Windsor & Wiehahn/The Image Bank/Getty Images

All Scripture is quoted from the Authorized King James Version.

The Man You Could Be
Paul W. Downey

Design by Nick Ng
Composition by Kelley Moore

© 2007 BJU Press
Greenville, SC 29609
JourneyForth Books is a division of BJU Press.

ISBN 978-1-59166-759-9
15 14 13 12 11 10 9 8 7 6 5 4 3 2

For Brittany and Brandon,
whose transformation from
children to godly young adults
has been a joy to behold.

May you steadfastly demonstrate
obedient faith as you continue
on the lifelong journey of
becoming the woman and
the man you could be.

Contents

Introduction

The thirteen lessons in this study are drawn from lessons that can be learned from the life of Joshua—the leader of ancient Israel who took over when Moses died. To complete this study, the only things you will need besides this book are your Bible, some time, and a willingness to be honest with yourself and God.

Each lesson in this book starts with a statement of the theme for that lesson, includes a verse or two to memorize that relates to the theme, and provides the reference to the section of the book of Joshua from which the lesson is drawn. Then comes the lesson itself, interspersed with questions for you to answer along the way. The hardest questions to answer will probably be the ones that require you to think about how the lesson applies to your life, especially when you find that there are things you need to change in order to become the kind of man God wants you to be. Each lesson ends with one or two projects that may take a little more time to complete.

In most cases, you should be able to do the reading and complete each lesson in less than an hour. If you really want to, you could complete the whole study in a couple of weeks by doing one lesson a day. I expect most students will prefer to take three months, doing one lesson a week. That will give you more time to answer the questions, memorize the verses, work on the projects, and think about how the material can be applied in your life.

You may be asking, "Why study Joshua?" I was introduced to many Old Testament heroes as a child in Sunday school. Joshua was one of my favorites. Stories about the crossing of Jordan and the collapse of the walls of Jericho stirred my heart with wonder.

My first intimate contact with this great book came shortly before my twenty-first birthday. I had just started my final semester in Bible college, working toward a bachelor's degree in music education, when I was assigned the task of teaching the book of Joshua to an eighth-grade Bible class as part of my student teaching responsibilities. I was to use nothing but the Bible for my text.

I can't say for sure how much I accomplished in the lives of my eighth-grade students years ago, but God did a work in my heart. By the end of the semester, I had developed a life-long love for teaching the Word, particularly the Old Testament historical narratives. I had set out to teach music, which I did for a while, but the Lord eventually took me into the pastorate and through three seminary degree programs.

Through the years it has been my joy to occasionally return to Joshua as a teaching text. I still find the stories exciting and the lessons rich. Joshua is the kind of man each of us should try to become. Even though it bears his name, the book of Joshua isn't really about Joshua as much as it's about God and His dealings with His people. *Its primary message is that for the Christian to enjoy the blessing of God in his life, he must be obedient to the instructions of God.*

In some ways, Joshua records a real-life application of the parallel truths of God's sovereignty and man's responsibility. You will often see tension between God's promises (that is, "I have given"—Joshua 6:2*b*) and His commands (that is, "ye shall"—Joshua 6:3*a**). God promises the believer many things, and those promises are guaranteed in Christ, on the basis of His finished work on the cross and His victory over death in the resurrection. But God expects the believer to obey.

The eternal life that can be yours in Christ does not depend on your earning it or keeping it—it is all a gift of God's grace. But the *obedient* believer can look forward to meeting the Savior and hearing Him say,

---

*The "a" or "b" following a verse number means to read either the first half or the second half of the verse.

"Well done, good and faithful servant" (Matthew 25:21, 23). Just as Israel had to depend on God and then walk obediently into the Jordan River, or depend on God and march repeatedly around the city of Jericho, believers today are to depend on Christ and live for Him.

It is my prayer for you that through studying how God worked in the life of this great man, you will learn to become "The Man You Could Be."

To the praise of the glory of Christ,

Paul W. Downey

Lesson 1
Becoming a Winner for God

*Spiritual victory is the only winning that really matters,
and that comes by believing God and doing what He says.*

Memory Verse: Joshua 1:8–9 "This book of the law shall not depart
out of thy mouth; but thou shalt meditate therein day
and night, that thou mayest observe to do according
to all that is written therein: for then thou shalt make
thy way prosperous, and then thou shalt have good
success. Have not I commanded thee? Be strong and
of a good courage; be not afraid, neither be thou dismayed: for the Lord thy God is with thee whitherso-
ever thou goest."

Bible Reading: Joshua 1:1–9

Not very many guys have the advantages of a good home environ-
ment, a good neighborhood, good schools, and good friends. Fewer
still enjoy great wealth. So how can an average guy emulate a great
leader like Joshua?

It helps to remember that Joshua wasn't always a powerful leader.
The first time we hear of him in Exodus 17:8–14, he was already
forty years old. Since that was just a few days or weeks after Moses
led Israel out of Egypt, one thing we know about him is that he had
grown up as a slave. The Bible tells us that the treatment of the
Hebrew slaves was especially harsh in the years leading up to God's
delivering them from Egypt. It's safe to assume that Joshua's first
forty years were not very pleasant.

Q: What are some circumstances in your life that feel like *disad-vantages* on the road to success?

A: _____

_____

Q: What are some circumstances in your life that might be *advantages* on the road to success?

A: _____

_____

We know that Joshua grew to manhood in a condition of slavery and political suppression. In a setting like that, many people would turn bitter and angry. But not Joshua. He learned important lessons of obedience and submission that would help him find obeying and serving God much more rewarding than serving his Egyptian masters had been.

There are times in life when you will be given a job or school assignment that seems to have no purpose. When you ask why you have to do this pointless task, do you resent it when you are told, "Because it builds character"? God's character-building program can be even tougher than your teacher's or your parents' or your boss's. Sometimes it involves a death in the family, your parents' divorce, or even abuse. You can begin to feel that *survival* is going to be difficult, and *success* in life is out of reach. That may well be how Joshua felt for the first forty years of his life. He had no idea what God had in store for him.

Joshua spent most of the next forty years of life as the understudy to Moses, helping him deal with the griping and complaining of the people of Israel as they worked their way toward the Promised Land. Joshua came from a generation that left Egypt in triumph, but then got scared and refused to trust God to keep His promise to give them victory over their enemies.

Q: When Israel said they would rather die in the wilderness (Numbers 14:2) than risk their lives trying to conquer Canaan, what did God tell them (Numbers 14:27–35)?

A: _____

_____

So Israel spent forty years camping in the Sinai desert. A lifetime of wandering in the wilderness in fear and disobedience describes the experience of many professing Christians, but it is not the way God wants Christians to live. During the years of Israel's wilderness wandering, Joshua and Caleb are the kind of men all believers are *supposed to be*. The rest of their generation illustrate what many believers *are*: fearful, wavering, disobedient, presumptuous, provocative, and eventually dead.

Q: In 1 Corinthians 3:1–4, what does Paul call that kind of Christian?

A: _____

_____

Q: In 1 Corinthians 11:28–32, what does Paul say might be the consequence of a believer's persistent disobedience?

A: _____

_____

Before he ever became the leader of Israel, Joshua had to learn many important lessons while serving under Moses. The first time he is mentioned is in the context of a battle.

Q: How do you think the event recorded in Exodus 17:8–14 taught Joshua the need for obedient faith?

A: _____

_____

The central lesson of Joshua is that *for the believer to enjoy the blessing of God in his life, he must obey God's instructions.* God promises the believer many things. Those promises are guaranteed in Christ on the basis of His finished work on the cross and His conquest of death in the resurrection. But God expects the believer, the born-again new creation in Christ, to *obey.* Believers are to depend on Christ and diligently live for Him. Spiritual victory comes through obedient faith. The believer who wants to defeat the enemies of his soul must believe God's promises and obey God's instructions. The eternal life that is ours in Christ doesn't depend on our earning it or keeping it—it is all a gift of God's grace (Ephesians 2:8–9). But the *obedient* believer can anticipate the reward of hearing his Savior say, "Well done" (Matthew 25:21, 23).

In the glimpses we have of him in the books of Moses, we learn a lot about Joshua's character. As we've already seen, Joshua is shown to be an obedient servant of God who knew from experience the importance of relying on God for victory (Exodus 17:8–14). He was a man of loyalty and prayer (Exodus 24:13–33:11). Before his introduction as the leader of Israel, he was best known as the respected and trusted leader of the tribe of Ephraim (Numbers 13:8–14:9) who was one of the twelve men chosen by Moses to spy out the land of Canaan.

Q: In describing the land of Canaan, what were the facts about which all twelve of the spies agreed (Numbers 13:26–29)?

A: _____

_____

Q: What was the difference between the report of Joshua and Caleb and that of the other ten spies (Numbers 13:30–33)?

A: _____

_____

_____

From these glimpses of Joshua's life while in training for leadership we can identify four important lessons that he learned that would be vital to his future success:

- Difficulties can be either occasions for defeat and failure or opportunities for victory and growth.
- God's promises are worth more than popular support.
- Size does not determine significance.
- We can and must trust God in every circumstance.

Q: How would you describe "obedient faith"?

A: _____

_____

Q: Briefly describe some challenge or obstacle you've had to face recently that really needed obedient faith in order to overcome it.

A: _____

_____

Q: What did you do?

A: _____

_____

Q: If you had it to do over again, what would you do differently in the light of the Bible?

A: _____

_____

Finally, after eighty years of preparation, Joshua was ready to assume leadership of Israel. In Joshua 1:1–9 God reveals two very similar traits that Joshua would have to exercise in order to successfully please God: *faith* and *faithfulness*. God's repeated command that Joshua trust Him without fear wasn't based on wishful thinking but on solid evidence that God was trustworthy. Joshua had learned from experience that even though God might order him to do things that seemed impossible, God would also enable him to do them. God didn't tell Joshua there would be no enemies to face, but that those enemies would surely be overcome by Joshua's and Israel's obedience.

Actually, God told Joshua that "the book of the law" was more important to Israel's success than Joshua was (Joshua 1:8). Studying and meditating on the Word of God would be absolutely necessary. Meditation involves carefully thinking about what God has said and applying His Word to your life. This won't happen by accident. Just reading a few verses in the morning or evening isn't going to cut it without careful thought about what the passage means and how God expects you to live.

Q: List a few things that God expects of you that you know you can't do on your own.

A: _____

_____

_____

Q: God said that the Bible was more important than the leader-ship of Joshua was. How do you think the supreme importance of God's Word should affect your attitudes?

A: _____

_____

_____

Without purposeful, dedicated study of God's Word and applica-tion of it to life's circumstances, challenges, and choices, you and I will surely fail. But God promises success if we will learn to obey.

Projects for Developing an Obedient Faith

1. While serving as Moses' assistant, Joshua learned four lessons vital to his future success (see page 5). Think of a practical way to demonstrate one or more of these truths to a friend or family member. Write out what you plan to do.

_____

_____

_____

_____

_____

_____

_____

2. List several things that sometimes interfere with, or keep you from, your Bible study and meditation on the Word. Then list some specific things you could do to safeguard your time and help you avoid distractions.

_____

_____

_____

_____

_____

_____

_____

Lesson 2
Putting on Your Game Face

Winning always requires focused effort. Spiritual victory takes preparation and determination to obey the Lord.

Memory Verse: 1 Peter 5:8–9*a* "Be sober, be vigilant; because your adversary the devil, as a roaring lion, walketh about, seeking whom he may devour: whom resist stedfast in the faith."

Bible Reading: Joshua 1:10–2:7

Have you ever paid attention to how top athletes approach a big game or significant competition? Take golf, for instance. When preparing for a tournament, especially one of the four "major" tournaments each year, most of the participants will arrive a few days early to practice on that golf course so they will know what to expect on each hole. They also work on getting focused on playing the four-round tournament one shot at a time—thinking about the shot they have to make right now without worrying about the bad shot they made earlier or what might happen on the next hole. Few are ever as focused as Tiger Woods, and many sports analysts attribute much of Tiger's success to his ability to shut out distractions and concentrate on the task at hand. You could say that he plays his best when he has put on his "game face."

Sometimes just getting out of bed in the morning can be terrifying. When a big job or hard responsibility looms in front of you, it's easy to make excuses and put it off. It's also tempting to plow ahead in life without much preparation or concentration. God doesn't want believers to be either rash or impulsive, but when He has given us clear instructions, He expects us to act and leave the consequences to Him. One reason I admire Joshua is that I see in him none of my native tendency to hesitate or procrastinate. When God gave him something to do, Joshua made no excuses and tolerated no delay. He focused on the task at hand, put on his game face, and got the job done.

Q: List a few things you've done or decisions you've made that were rash (risky) or impulsive (emotionally driven) that proved to be not too smart.

A: _____

_____

Q: List a few things you know God wants you to do (or stop doing) that you haven't really worked on like you should.

A: _____

_____

For Joshua, obedience was sometimes complicated by the fact that God didn't always give him detailed instructions on how to accomplish what God told him to do. Joshua's first big task was to get Israel across the Jordan River into Canaan. While Joshua had no idea what Israel would need to cross the river, he knew they would need strength for whatever challenges they might face. So, instead of risking a waste of resources busily making things like boats and rafts that they may not need, he told Israel to get ready for the crossing by preparing *food* ("victuals" in the KJV). Where would they get this food? It was the manna that God had been providing for a generation.

Some challenges to our faith we may see coming, so we can have a pretty good idea how to deal with them. Others come as surprise attacks. Actually, none of us knows what spiritual dangers may confront us on any given day. Joshua's example shows us how to prepare: we must feed on the milk and meat of God's Word (1 Peter 2:2; Hebrews 5:12–13). Great feats of spiritual strength—like Israel's faith to walk through the river or your faith to obey the Lord despite hard circumstances—require spiritual nourishment only God can provide.

Q: Briefly describe a time recently when you were faced with a spiritual challenge.

A: _____

_____

Q: Explain why you believe you were well prepared for that challenge, or what you could do to be better prepared for the next unexpected challenge you face.

A: _____

_____

It's easy for Christians of any age to be really *busy* with spiritual activities without being adequately *prepared* for spiritual battles. You may expect your church's youth ministry to provide lots of fun activities without ever thinking much about the need to be instructed or taught. You need to remember that the most important thing your church can do for you, or for anyone else, is to help you be properly fed for the spiritual conflicts that will bombard you from day to day (Acts 20:28–30; Ephesians 4:11–13; 1 Timothy 5:17; 2 Timothy 2:2; 3:16–17).

Still, we see that Joshua knew that *faith doesn't take the place of duty.* That is, just because you believe God will help you does not mean you no longer have to work at obeying. When preparing to cross the Jordan, Joshua reminded the tribes of Reuben, Gad, and Manasseh of Moses' promise that they would receive the land on the east side of the river. He also reminded them of their obligation to lead the rest of Israel in the conquest of the land on the west side of the river (Joshua 1:12–15). In issuing his orders, he told them they should do this out of gratitude to God and love for their brethren, but he emphasized that their most important motive must be obedience. They were to lead the way into Canaan because God expected it of them.

For instance, it is pretty obvious that in our society today many teens are sexually active. That has caused a lot of people to call for abstinence education. Teaching young men and women to abstain from sexual activity before they are married is both biblical and vital. But most of the instruction given on the need for sexual abstinence encourages you to wait until you *are ready* on the basis of your self-worth. You are being encouraged to maintain your virginity on the basis of pride ("you are worth waiting for") or on the basis of fear ("you could get a disease"). The problem is that people who wait on the basis of pride will eventually get sexually involved when they decide it suits them, and people who wait on the basis of fear will engage in sexual activity when they believe it is safe. They have been told their most important concern is either pleasing themselves or protecting themselves. But the only proper motive for sexual purity is that God demands it. No other reason has any real authority, because it is based on how you feel.

Q: Why is sex wrong outside of marriage (Exodus 20:14; Galatians 5:19–21)?

A: _____

_____

Q: Why is cheating on your homework wrong (Exodus 20:15; Ephesians 4:25)?

A: _____

_____

Q: Why is using profanity wrong (Exodus 20:7; Ephesians 4:29)?

A: _____

_____

Q: Why should you obey your parents (Exodus 20:12; Ephesians 6:1–3)?

A: _____

_____

Q: Why should you witness to your unsaved friends (Matthew 28:18–20)?

A: _____

_____

Q: Why should your unsaved friend believe the gospel and be saved (Acts 17:30)?

A: _____

_____

Your obedience must not be determined by how you feel—you should obey God whether or not you feel like it. On the night before He was crucified, the Lord Jesus said to His disciples, "If ye love me, keep my commandments" (John 14:15). That command, by itself, would be scary—the only way to prove our love for the Lord is to do everything He says. Just a few verses later, Jesus explained that the power to obey would come from Him. He said, "I am the vine, ye are the branches: He that abideth in me, and I in him, the same bringeth forth much fruit: for without me ye can do nothing" (John 15:5). Thankfully, God enables us to do everything He commands us to do.

Q: What does Philippians 2:12–13 teach us about the relationship between obedience and God's help?

A: _____

_____

For you to become the man you could be, you must believe what God has promised, pay attention to what God gives you to do, and focus on what He says. The way to victory is to be prepared for the task and dedicated to fulfilling it. Like Tiger Woods preparing for an important golf tournament and Joshua preparing to face an enemy army, you have to "put on your game face" and serve the Lord.

PROJECT FOR DEVELOPING AN OBEDIENT FAITH

The Bible often tells us that we can experience spiritual victory only if we know the Word of God and determine to obey it. To help you remember this principle, look up the five passages listed below and write them out.

Psalm 119:2–3 _____

_____

_____

_____

Psalm 119:9 _____

_____

_____

_____

Psalm 119:105 _____

_____

_____

_____

John 14:15 _____

_____

_____

_____

2 Timothy 3:16–17 _____

_____

_____

_____

Lesson 3
Whom Can You Trust?

God brings circumstances into your life to teach
you to trust Him, and others will be able to see the
effects of your faith in the way you live your life.

Memory Verse: Hebrews 11:1 and 31 "Now faith is the substance of things hoped for, the evidence of things not seen. . . . By faith the harlot Rahab perished not with them that believed not, when she had received the spies with peace."

Bible Reading: Joshua 2:8–24

Before Israel crossed the Jordan River into Canaan, Joshua appointed two spies to enter Jericho and bring back any information they could gather on the situation they found there (Joshua 2:1–3). You may be surprised to discover that the spies ended up staying in the house of a prostitute named Rahab. Even more surprising, we find that God had directed them to Rahab's home because He intended to save her. Why? Obviously not because she was a good person. God was working to save Rahab for the same reason He is willing to save you or me—God delights to show grace to the undeserving.

God's plans for Rahab weren't obvious to the spies. While most of Israel was back in camp preparing food for the crossing, these two men were cornered in enemy territory, having been discovered on the first day in the city. Things were not going well. Not only was it likely that they had failed their mission, but they may well lose their lives. When the king of Jericho sent men to arrest them, amazingly, Rahab hid them on the roof.

This incident teaches us a lot about trust. The spies had to trust Rahab, and Rahab chose to trust the spies, but they were all trusting God. Rahab's actions proved that she had turned her back on her old life and identified with Israel. She cut her ties to her Canaanite gods and the Canaanite people, having decided to trust the one true God.

Q: How does what the Lord Jesus says in Luke 14:26 relate to Rahab's actions?

A: _____

_____

Q: When Paul was explaining his ministry to King Agrippa, he said that he had preached "that they should repent and turn to God, and do works meet for repentance" (Acts 26:19–20). How does what Paul said apply to Rahab's choice to protect the Israelite spies?

A: _____

_____

Rahab's sudden and total change of loyalties is exactly what the Bible means by "repentance" when we are told to repent and turn to the Lord Jesus. Like Rahab, you cannot be saved by trying to be good, but neither can you be saved without a change of loyalty. What is involved in changing from being God's enemy, like Rahab was, to being a member of His family, like Rahab became? In the section below, look up the verses and summarize in your own words answers to the questions presented.

Q: Who is God (Revelation 4:11; Genesis 1:26–27)?

A: _____

_____

Q: Who are you (Acts 17:24–26, 31)?

A: _____

_____

Q: What did Adam do wrong (Genesis 3:1–13)?

A: _____

_____

Q: What was the consequence of that sin (Genesis 3:14–23;
1 Corinthians 15:21–22)?

A: _____

_____

Q: Why is that a problem for you (Romans 3:10–12, 23; 1 John 3:4)?

A: _____

_____

Q: What is the penalty for sinning against God (Romans 6:23)?

A: _____

_____

Q: There are three kinds of death described in the Bible, and all
result from sin. Match the following Bible verses to the kind of
death to which it refers: Hebrews 9:27; Revelation 20:14b–15;
Ephesians 2:1.

Spiritual death _____

Physical death _____

Eternal death _____

Q: What can you do to earn eternal life and avoid the eternal death of damnation (Proverbs 14:12; Titus 3:5)?

A: _____

_____

Q: Is there any way to find eternal life in God (Romans 6:23; Ephesians 2:8–9; Acts 16:31)?

A: _____

_____

Q: What do the following passages tell us about Who Jesus is and how He can help?

  1. John 1:3 and Colossians 1:16–17

  _____

  _____

  2. Luke 1:30–35

  _____

  _____

  3. Romans 5:18 and 1 Peter 3:18a

  _____

  _____

  4. 1 Corinthians 15:3b–4, 17, 20–22

  _____

  _____

Q: How do you receive God's pardon for your sin (John 14:6; Acts 3:19a; 16:31a; Romans 10:13)?

A: _____

_____

Q: What has God promised you if you believe (John 5:24)?

A: _____

_____

Q: Have you been born again, repented of sin, and turned your life over to Jesus Christ as your Lord and Savior?

A: _____

_____

If not, will you do so today? To become a Christian, you must admit that you have sinned against God and deserve His punishment, and you must ask Him to forgive you. You must believe that the Lord Jesus Christ is the Son of God Who died for you, rose from the dead, and is the living Lord of all creation. You must call upon Jesus Christ to be your Lord and Savior.

While Israel was still camped across the Jordan River, Rahab committed herself to forsake her people and become an Israelite. That took a lot of courage and faith. She was convinced that she and her people faced immediate, inevitable destruction. When Israel's spies showed up at her door, she didn't panic, and she didn't turn them in to the authorities. Incredibly, she decided they represented her only hope.

Later, in Joshua 6:25, we find Rahab being rescued during the destruction of Jericho and being brought into the camp of Israel. Later still (Matthew 1:5), we discover that she married into the tribe of Judah and became one of the ancestors of Jesus Christ. God's grace is truly amazing!

Read what Rahab said to the spies in Joshua 2:9–11, then read what Israel said in response to the report of the twelve spies forty years earlier in Numbers 14:1–4.

Q: What happened to the Israelites who chose to trust men rather than God (Numbers 14:28–29)?

A: _____

_____

Q: What happened to the Canaanite woman (Rahab) who chose to trust God rather than man?

A: _____

_____

Q: What does this teach you about whom you should trust?

A: _____

_____

Rahab's faith is especially remarkable given how little she knew about God, but her actions proved that her faith was genuine (Hebrews 11:31). Her protection of the spies proved that God had changed her heart and that she had chosen to be identified with Him and His people. Any claim to faith that can't be seen in a changed life, new loyalties, and altered goals is useless. Real faith works. If it doesn't work, it isn't faith—it's just wishful thinking. Rahab believed that Israel's God was good and powerful, and that was enough for her. She put her life in the hands of two men she'd never seen before and might never see again. She risked everything and withheld nothing. While in some ways Rahab's faith was meager and uninformed, it was genuine because its source and object was the one true God (Hebrews 12:2). Her actions did not make her a convert—they proved she was a new creature.

Q: What goals, attitudes, and behavior have changed in your life since you were saved?

A: _____

_____

Q: What are some things that still need to change?

A: _____

_____

When Rahab asked the spies to promise to protect her family, she put them in something of a bind. God had forbidden Israel to make covenants, or treaties, with the people of Canaan (Deuteronomy 7:2). However, God had ordered the destruction of the Canaanites because they were idolaters and had rejected God. When Rahab voluntarily sided with Israel and Israel's God, she was no longer under the ban of judgment. She was eligible for protection and could even participate in the blessings God promised His people.

Because of Rahab's demonstration of faith, the spies promised to spare Rahab and her family if she would not reveal their mission. They gave her two instructions to guarantee that they would all keep their promises. First, she must hang a scarlet rope out of the window of her house on the wall of the city. Second, she must be sure that any member of her family or household that wanted to join her in Israel stayed inside that house when the city fell. Practically, this would make it possible for Israel to identify the home they had promised to protect. Spiritually, this illustrated that salvation is through the blood of Christ and that those who are in Christ are safe and secure.

Rahab didn't wait until Israel's army showed up at Jericho's gates to hang the scarlet cord out the window. She left if there from that day forward. She wanted there to be no doubt in the minds of Israel that she was committed to their cause. This was no half-hearted conversion under pressure—which isn't really a conversion anyway. This was denying herself, taking up her "cross," and following (Matthew 16:24) that proved that God had really changed her heart.

Q: What does the fact that God was willing to save a Canaanite prostitute and even bless her by making her an ancestor of Jesus Christ prove about God's grace (Ephesians 2:8–10)?

A: _____

_____

Q: How might that apply to you?

A: _____

_____

PROJECTS FOR DEVELOPING AN OBEDIENT FAITH

1. List any family members, friends, or acquaintances you know who need a gospel witness. Pray for wisdom and courage to speak with them and begin looking for opportunities to point them toward the Savior. Set realistic target dates by which you hope to have been able to speak with them about their need of salvation.

_____

_____

_____

2. Write out the story of your conversion. Include an account of how God worked out circumstances to lead you to faith, how you responded to the gospel, and the impact it has had on your life so far.

_____

_____

_____

_____

_____

Lesson 4
When the Going Gets Tough

*God wants to provide everything you need to get
through any challenge He allows into your life, but
first you have to admit that you need Him.*

Memory Verse: 1 Corinthians 10:13 "There hath no temptation taken
you but such as is common to man: but God is faith-
ful, who will not suffer you to be tempted above that
ye are able; but will with the temptation also make a
way to escape, that ye may be able to bear it."

Bible Reading: Joshua 3:1–17

Life is full of obstacles of one kind or another. While I am sure
that Joshua and the people of Israel were eager to finally enter the
Promised Land, they probably felt at least a little dread over what
faced them. On the verge of moving into the land, at the height of
their excitement over the fulfillment of God's promise, there were
still obstacles to overcome. The first one they had to deal with
was the flooded Jordan River. Joshua 3 tells the story of how Israel
crossed the Jordan.

Joshua knew there was no way around this obstacle. He "rose early
in the morning" (Joshua 3:1) and started Israel moving toward the
challenge. How different from the way many of us deal with our
problems! Most of us would rather put off confronting our problems or even try to avoid them altogether. Joshua ordered Israel to
move their camp about ten miles, bringing everyone within sight of
the river. It's one thing to hear about a challenge you have to overcome, but it's something else altogether to have to stare it in the

face. Showing Israel just how overwhelming this task was, God was proving to them that they needed Him. He brought them to the end of their resources before He started working on their behalf.

Q: Read Psalm 107:5, 12, 18, and 27. What did the people described in each of these verses have in common?

A: _____

_____

Q: Now read Psalm 107:6, 13, 19, and 28. In each case, what happened?

A: _____

_____

After spending three days staring at the impassible Jordan River, Joshua turned Israel's attention from the trouble toward the solution. He told them to look to the ark of the covenant, which stood for the presence of God among them (Joshua 3:3). The stone tablets on which the Ten Commandments were engraved were inside the ark. The lid of the ark was called the mercy seat. In order to leave the wilderness and move into the Promised Land, Israel would have to follow God's law covered by His mercy—practicing obedient faith.

One truth this illustrates is the relationship between law and grace, which many Christians misunderstand. No one is ever saved by obeying the law of God. It is not possible. If we could do that, the Son of God did not need to become a man and die for our sins. Since we can't perfectly obey the Law, the *Lord Jesus* obeyed it for us. God's mercy and grace credits Christ's perfect righteousness to those who believe on Him. That is, when someone is born again through faith in Jesus Christ, God cancels out all of his sin on the basis of the perfect obedience of Jesus. He counts Jesus' obedience as if it had been ours and lets Jesus' death pay for our sin. This sets us free from the law of sin and death (Romans 8:2) and makes it possible for us to obey Him by faith (Romans 9:30–31; 1 John 2:6). We are saved on the basis of Christ's obedience and His blood sacrifice in our place, which God's grace applies to our account through faith.

Q: Explain in your own words what Ephesians 2:8–10 means.

A: _____

_____

Another truth illustrated in Joshua 3 is the proper attitude we should display of reverence for God. Other than the priests who were told to carry the ark, no one was to approach any closer to it than a little over half a mile (Joshua 3:4). The better our grasp of Who God is, the greater will be our reverence before Him.

Q: Hebrews 4:16 says, "Let us therefore come boldly unto the throne of grace." What do you think this means about your access to God?

A: _____

_____

Q: What is the significance of the use of the word *throne* in this verse?

A: _____

_____

Q: Why should we remember that this is a "throne of *grace*"?

A: _____

_____

Israel had come to a point where they needed to push the limits of their faith. They would need the miraculous intervention of God to cross the Jordan. Relaying God's instructions, Joshua told the priests carrying the ark to march into the water and "stand still in Jordan" while the rest of Israel crossed the river (Joshua 3:7–8). What Joshua describes in the rest of chapter 3 is absolutely amazing! As the priests walked into the river, God cut off the water flowing into the river at a point many miles to the north. The water above the cut-off point "rose up upon an heap" (literally, "congealed," or became like Jell-o), while the water below it flowed on toward the

Dead Sea to the south. The water at the feet of the priests carrying the ark gradually receded. By the time the rest of the Israelites got there from their half-mile following distance, the river bed was completely dry. They were able to walk across the river bed without getting wet or dirty. Joshua says that when they came up on the opposite bank, they were all "clean" (Joshua 3:17).

When we think about how Israel was told to follow the ark of the covenant, we learn something of what God expects of His people—not to become His people, but because we are His people. In Israel's crossing of the river, we see God demonstrating His almighty power as He removes the most daunting of obstacles—and He does it without fanfare or spectacle. We also see how we should act when facing a difficult or dangerous situation, calmly following God's instructions and trusting Him to do His will.

The New Testament was originally written in Greek and has been translated into English. In the memory verse for this lesson the phrase translated "a way to escape" sounds like it means that God is promising you a way out of your problems. However, in the original Greek the verse actually promises that God will make "the way through" your trials and temptations.

Q: Explain in your own words what 1 Corinthians 10:13 means.

A: _____

_____

Q: How do you think this verse might apply to some specific challenge you are facing now or have dealt with recently?

A: _____

_____

You and I shouldn't flinch from the floodwaters of life. Sometimes we face situations that threaten to overwhelm us, but God is always with us. We may want to run in the opposite direction, but God doesn't permit us to retreat. He doesn't want us to try to find a way around those obstacles either. He doesn't even want us to try to blast our way through them on our own. He expects us to trust Him to take us safely through them. God never promises that life won't be frightening or hard. He promises it will be bearable if we will obey Him and trust Him.

Q: Read Psalm 3 and explain how it relates to this subject.

A: _____

_____

The old cliché says, "When the going gets tough, the tough get going." It is a clever play on words, but it teaches self-reliance rather than reliance on God. The Bible actually teaches, "When the going gets tough, the righteous trust God and keep going."

PROJECTS FOR DEVELOPING AN OBEDIENT FAITH

1. In Lesson 1 you were asked to list a few things that God expects of you that you know you can't do on you own. Briefly describe where you stand with those situations or matters now.

_____

_____

_____

_____

_____

_____

_____

_____

_____

_____

_____

2. Write out the stories of at least one or two situations you have faced in which God brought you through a trial that seemed at the time as if it would overwhelm you. These stories along with the account of your conversion that you wrote in Lesson 3 will be important for your present and future encouragement. They will also help you be prepared to share your testimony with others.

_____

_____

_____

_____

_____

_____

_____

_____

_____

_____

_____

_____

_____

_____

_____

_____

_____

_____

_____

_____

Lesson 5
"Me, a Role Model?"

God expects you to set a good example for anyone
who may be watching, always giving Him the
credit for being your Savior and Guide.

Memory Verse: 1 Timothy 4:12 "Let no man despise thy youth; but be thou an example of the believers, in word, in conversation, in charity, in spirit, in faith, in purity."

Bible Reading: Joshua 4:1–5:12

Years ago I was listening to a missionary give a report about his ministry in Japan when he made a point I've never forgotten. He said, "An unsaved person has every right to look at anyone who calls himself a 'Christian' and expect to find the answer to his every need." Think about that a minute. If you are going to apply to yourself a name that means "Christ-like-one," you'd better look a lot like Christ. Since you may be the best picture of God that your neighbor, teacher, friend, or relative will ever see, it's important to make that image lifelike. If you and I expect to witness effectively to the world around us, they'd better be able to see in us an accurate picture of Christ.

One of the most important characteristics of any positive role model is consistency. A person can live consistently only if he has a pretty clear idea what he is supposed to do and develops the habit of keeping his mind focused on it. We all need some means of keeping ourselves focused on who we are in Christ and what we are to do for

Him. Building in reminders can be very important to keep us from forgetting what *role* we are to *model* before others.

For Israel under Joshua, crossing through the Jordan River represented entering into judgment and emerging cleansed. Israel's crossing moved them from their former lives in the wilderness to their new lives in the Promised Land. In a sense, it pictured what being born again by the Holy Spirit does for the child of God in transforming a person from being dead in trespasses and sins to being alive in Christ.

In the opening verses of Joshua 4 we find that one representative from each of the twelve tribes of Israel was to take a stone from the dry riverbed to the new camp at Gilgal on the other side. These stones were to be built into a monument that would be a sign among the Israelites, reminding them of this miraculous event and of God's promise of future blessing in the land. God had representatives from each tribe do this, because He wanted everyone in Israel to identify with this project. Building the memorial was not something done for them by the priests. It was something in which the people were involved and in which each person had a stake.

Although the people's representatives carried the stones from the riverbed, it was Joshua who built the monument from those stones. This demonstrated that Israel came together as a unit by following their God-appointed leader.

Q: How was Joshua's building of the memorial monument a picture of the work of Jesus Christ, the Head of the church (Ephesians 4:1–16)?

A: _____

_____

Joshua also built a monument in the middle of the river, where the priests had stood. When God released the waters, and the Jordan returned to flood stage, this monument would have been overwhelmed. This would picture Christ Jesus' bearing the judgment of

God in our place, while the monument on the shore pictured His having delivered us from judgment safe and sound.

Since a memorial is not much use if nobody knows what it means, Joshua told the men of Israel that they would have to use the monument at the new camp as a tool to teach each new generation what God had done. There were three ways the memorial was to be a sign. First, it would signify that Israel could not have crossed Jordan except by God's power—for the stones to have come from the riverbed, God had to stop the river's flow.

Q: How does the cross of Christ demonstrate this truth for us (Romans 5:6)?

A: _____

_____

The second thing the memorial would signify is that Israel had crossed the river unmarked—they had come through judgment unharmed.

Q: How does the cross of Christ demonstrate this truth for us (Romans 5:8–9; 8:1)?

A: _____

_____

Thirdly, the memorial signified God's promise of future blessing—having brought them this far, He would not fail to keep all of His Word.

Q: How does the cross of Christ demonstrate this truth for us (Romans 8:29–31)?

A: _____

_____

Many generations later, John the Baptist was teaching and baptizing in the Jordan River near Jericho. It is almost certainly this very monument to which he referred in Matthew 3:9—"God is able of these stones to raise up children unto Abraham."

Q: If we assume that John the Baptist and Joshua were both making the same point, what do you think John meant?

A: _____

_____

God's works are worth recording and remembering. If we don't set up some kind of marker or record what He has done in some way, we are almost certainly going to forget. You've probably never experienced anything as spectacular as the parting of the Red Sea or the drying up of the Jordan River. Neither have I. Still, God's providential direction of your life and mine has been just as real, if usually more subtle. God wants you to become the man you can be, a Christian whose faith is solid and whose life is a testimony of God's grace. Don't be surprised if some of the things God takes you through to accomplish that are painful or even downright terrifying. If we never faced difficulties, we'd quickly forget that we need God, and we'd never learn to trust Him.

Q: What are some ways God has directed in your life to bring you to where you are today?

A: _____

_____

Q: What can you do to help you remember some of the things God has done in directing your life and providing for you?

A: _____

_____

Peter says something about being a role model in 1 Peter 3:15—"But sanctify the Lord God in your hearts: and be ready always to give an answer to every man that asketh you a reason of the hope that is in you with meekness and fear." When he says "sanctify the

Lord God in your hearts," he means that we are to give our hearts completely to God as our Lord and Master. We are to let Him rule our lives. Then we are to be ready to explain why we are living in obedience to God.

Q: Are there attitudes, activities, or associations in your life that might make people wonder if you've really been saved by the grace of God? If so, what are they?

A: _____

_____

Q: What can you do to make your life a better picture of God and His grace?

A: _____

_____

You may be thinking, "I could never be a role model." Maybe you think you are too young and the responsibility is just too great. The Bible never tells us that it is OK to live any way we want when we are kids or teens, as if we would magically become good Christians on our eighteenth or twenty-first birthdays. Many great men of God in the Bible dedicated themselves to serving Him when they were young. Joseph was serving God faithfully for years before his brothers sold him as a slave when he was sixteen. David was known as a godly young man when he was in his teens or younger. Daniel was taken captive by King Nebuchadnezzar and purposed in his heart to not defile himself when he was probably only thirteen or fourteen. Samuel was a dedicated servant of the Lord in the tabernacle when he was only six or seven.

Q: How does Paul's instruction to Timothy in this lesson's memory verse (1 Timothy 4:12) apply to you?

A: _____

_____

Q: How does Solomon's counsel in Ecclesiastes 12:1, 13, and 14 apply to you?

A: _____

_____

The truth is, all of us are role models, whether we want to be or not. Somebody is always watching. It may be a classmate, a brother or sister, a cousin, a neighbor, or a friend. It may be someone you never imagined would be watching you, like a teacher, a parent, or someone you don't even know at church or school. Since someone, somewhere, is learning how to act by watching you, it is important that you be a *good* role model. Being a good role model involves knowing what God has done for you, living in such a way that others can tell by watching you that you trust God, and being ready to explain what God has done for you whenever you get an opportunity.

Project for Developing an Obedient Faith

If we want other people to know God, we need to be ready to tell them about His works of grace in our own lives. One of the questions in this lesson asked you to list a few of the ways God's direction has been evident in your life. Spend some additional time thinking about how God has brought you through some challenge, prepared you for some task, strengthened you in some difficulty, or provided for you in some time of need. Write out some of the stories to help you prepare for telling other people about your faith in God.

_____

_____

_____

_____

_____

_____

_____

Lesson 6
What Makes a Hero?

*Great victories of faith that come from God involve
steadfast obedience more than spectacular effort.*

Memory Verse: Philippians 2:12*b*–13 "Work out your own salvation
with fear and trembling. For it is God which worketh
in you both to will and to do of his good pleasure."

Bible Reading: Joshua 5:13–6:27

Israel had arrived! They had crossed the river and set up camp in
the Promised Land. Life would now be simple, right? Wrong! Now
that they were in the land, they would have to conquer it. Canaan
was full of people who didn't want to leave and would fight back as
Israel moved in. Not only did the Canaanites have armies, but many
of them also lived in fortresses.

One of the reasons we think of Joshua as a hero is his great victory at Jericho. As Israel celebrated Passover week, the army stayed
in camp recovering from their recent circumcision (Joshua 5:2–12).
Knowing that as soon as the Passover observances ended it would
be time for Israel to start moving into Canaan, Joshua was probably a little restless. Jericho was the biggest, most strongly fortified
Canaanite city guarding the lower Jordan River valley, and it was
less than two miles from Israel's camp at Gilgal. It would have to be
conquered before Israel could push any farther into the land.

Israel's experiences in Canaan actually have a lot in common with
the Christian life. Having your sins forgiven and becoming a child
of God gave you peace with God. At the same time, it probably made

you a lot of new enemies. Some of those enemies are old friends and acquaintances, but some of the most dangerous of your new enemies are the sins in your own life that you now have to fight against and destroy.

Q: What are some battles you have won over temptation and sin in your life since you were saved?

A: _____

_____

Q: What are some of the "fortified cities" you still need to conquer in order to be fully obedient to Christ?

A: _____

_____

God had been very specific about Joshua's objective—to take the land. He'd not been at all specific about *how* he was supposed to do that. The book of the law that was to be Joshua's guide (Joshua 1:8) did not give him step-by-step instructions on how to take a heavily fortified city. So Joshua slipped out of camp alone to find a place from which he could observe Jericho's impressive fortifications.

As he pondered his options, Joshua was confronted by a soldier who was armed for battle and ready to fight with his sword already drawn. Even though he had no reason to expect this man to be anyone but an enemy, Joshua didn't run away, and he didn't attack. He confronted the man with a question: "Are you for us or for our adversaries?" Imagine Joshua's confusion when the armed soldier answered, "No." The man then explained that he had come "as captain of the host of the Lord." As the conversation continued, the Captain revealed that He was actually the Lord (Joshua 6:2). The point He was making to Joshua was that the real question was not whose side the Lord was on, but whether Joshua was fighting for the Lord or for His enemies.

When you are frustrated and scared because you face an enemy or obstacle you don't know how to handle, it is tempting to ask God,

"Whose side are you on anyway?" You have to remember that for you to have God on your side, you have to be on His side.

Think about some of those battles you are facing. Pause for a few minutes to pray, asking God for direction, for courage, for character, or for whatever you need to give you victory over temptation and sin today.

Q: Do you believe God wants you to do right?

A: _____

_____

Q: Do you believe God will help you do right?

A: _____

_____

With no heavy weapons and no experience at siege warfare, taking Jericho wouldn't be easy. Joshua had no idea how to breach the walls for taking the city. That is why it probably came as a great relief to discover that the Lord had a plan. To prove his loyalty to the Lord, Joshua was expected to follow God's instructions to the letter. The problem was that the details of God's plan were pretty bizarre.

Joshua was to assemble the whole army of Israel, some 530,000 men, to lead the way to Jericho. They were to be followed by a tiny group of seven priests with rams' horns leading the four priests who carried the ark. Behind them would follow the rest of the people of Israel. They would march to Jericho, march once around the city, then return to camp. They would do this in absolute silence every day for six days. On the seventh day they were to march around the city seven times, after which the priests would blow the rams' horns, the army would shout, and they would take the city.

The instructions were clear, but they didn't make much sense. As a military strategy it sounded ridiculous. That was the point. *Israel would not win the battle because of their superior strategy but because they followed a superior God.* Joshua didn't care that the instructions were strange. They had come from God, and he would do what he was told.

Q: Read 2 Corinthians 10:3–4. In our battle against sin and temptation ("the flesh"), what kind of weapons does Paul say will not be successful?

A: _____

_____

Q: How does he describe the spiritual weapons we are supposed to use?

A: _____

_____

Q: In the list below, mark with an "F" those methods of dealing with problems that would be "fleshly" and wrong and with an "S" those that would be "spiritual" and right.

_____ Getting mad and storming away

_____ Seeking advice from unsaved friends

_____ Asking for help from your parents, pastor, or Sunday school teacher

_____ Spending time reading the Bible and praying

_____ Skipping school to avoid the problem

_____ Getting more active in church and Christian ministry

_____ Developing habits that would avoid temptation

_____ Hanging out with friends that you know are not right with God

Q: How do you think you should deal with whatever problems you are facing right now?

A: _____

_____

In Joshua 6:2, just before explaining this odd battle strategy to Joshua, the Lord told him, "See, I have given into thine hand Jericho, and the king thereof, and the mighty men of valor." God was guaranteeing victory, but He was also requiring Joshua's obedience.

Q: How do you think this principle would apply to the problems you are facing?

A: _____

_____

I wonder if by the end of Israel's fourth or fifth day of marching around Jericho some Israelites had begun to doubt the effectiveness of this plan. No cracks had appeared in the walls. No representative from Jericho had volunteered to surrender. Had there been any point in mustering everyone in the camp for the five-mile daily march? Yes. Israel's accomplishment during those six days had less to do with conquering Jericho than with honoring God by their faith and obedience. Then, on the seventh day, after a march of perhaps twenty miles as they circled the city seven times, they were expected to shout out a victory cry while the walls were still standing. What faith!

The Bible tells us that after the priests blew the rams' horns and the people shouted, the walls "fell down flat," and the army advanced into the city. The fighting that day was brutal. Joshua records that they "utterly destroyed" every person and animal within the city with the exception of those protected by the promise made to Rahab. The spies she had protected were sent to rescue her and those with her from the slaughter, taking them back to a place just outside their camp in Gilgal.

Q: What do you think the following statement means?

"Israel's accomplishment during the first six days marching around Jericho had less to do with conquering the city than with honoring God by their faith and obedience."

A: _____

_____

Q: Why do you think the walls of Jericho fell that day?

A: _____

_____

Q: How do you think this principle might apply in your life?

A: _____

_____

Joshua became a hero in Israel at the battle of Jericho, not by using mighty weapons of war, but by the quiet, steady plodding of an obedient walk around the city. Heroes for God are not usually the ones that make a lot of noise and get a lot of attention. They are the people who steadily, faithfully, keep obeying God. Sometimes it is easy, but most of the time it isn't. You have to make up your mind to do the quiet things for God that are often unnoticed by others—like read your Bible, pray, and resist temptation—honoring God with your time and your life. When you do, those sins and temptations in your life that look like fortified cities impossible to defeat will collapse before you by God's power in response to your steady obedience.

PROJECT FOR DEVELOPING AN OBEDIENT FAITH

Think of one or two people you know who are finding it hard to obey God in a situation in which they don't seem to be making any progress. Begin to pray for them and to ask the Lord to help you find a way to encourage them.

_____

_____

_____

_____

_____

Lesson 7
You Are Not Invincible

Everybody, including you, is capable of
giving in to sinful temptation that can have
devastating effects on yourself and others.

Memory Verse: James 1:14–15 "But every man is tempted, when he is drawn away of his own lust, and enticed. Then when lust hath conceived, it bringeth forth sin: and sin, when it is finished, bringeth forth death."

Bible Reading: Joshua 7:1–26

In Joshua 6:17–19, Joshua had made it clear to all of Israel that everything in Jericho was dedicated to God. The gold, silver, brass, and iron were to be salvaged and turned over to the priests in charge of the tabernacle treasury. Everything else was to be burned.

God had demanded this of Israel to demonstrate the principle of the tithe—giving to God at least the first 10 percent of your income. Giving God the goods from the first city they conquered illustrated the fact that all things belong to God. It forced Israel to prove that they believed that Jericho was just a start—God would give them the rest of the land and allow them to keep the spoils from the rest of the cities, but the stuff from the first city went completely and totally to God. Israel was honoring God with the first of their "increase" and giving Him the glory for the victory over Jericho.

Centuries after Joshua had died, the prophet Malachi delivered the message of God to the nation of Israel. Read what he said in Malachi 3:8–12.

Q: Malachi accused Israel of robbing God because they hadn't done what (Malachi 3:8)?

A: _____

_____

Q: What did he say was true of those who were guilty (Malachi 3:9)?

A: _____

_____

Q: In Malachi 3:10, what did He promise if they would obey?

A: _____

_____

Q: What do you think God's promise in Malachi 3:11 means?

A: _____

_____

Q: Do you have a regular source of income, either from an allowance or a job?

A: _____

_____

Q: Is tithing, giving at least 10 percent to God by giving to your church, something you are in the habit of doing?

A: _____

_____

The seventh chapter of Joshua is the saddest in the book. There is sin in Israel, and Joshua hasn't noticed. A guy named Achan had kept some of the stuff from Jericho and hidden it in his tent. Joshua had no idea. Had Joshua known that God was angry with Israel for violating His command to keep nothing from Jericho for themselves, this episode would have developed a lot differently. Joshua decided to go ahead and attack the neighboring city of Ai on the basis of the information at hand, and the consequences were disastrous.

The adage "Strike while the iron is hot" is usually good advice. Armies like to press the attack while they have the advantage. Taking a break after a victory can give the enemy time to regroup and recover, and may squander what my high school basketball coach used to call "the big MO"—momentum. Sometimes, though, getting in a hurry can cause you to make some pretty serious mistakes. Overconfidence can lead to reckless enthusiasm that can leave you wide open to attack and shift the momentum back to your opponent.

Joshua looked at Jericho, the region's strongest fortress, and saw nothing but a smoldering ruin. The neighboring town of Ai was small and weak. If Jericho was a Rottweiller, Ai was a Chihuahua. But even an angry Chihuahua can be a nuisance if ignored. Not content to stop to celebrate one big victory, Joshua sent men to check out the situation in Ai. When they returned, they told Joshua he should send only two or three thousand men against that city, letting the bulk of the exhausted army of Israel rest.

Incredibly, the three thousand men Joshua dispatched to Ai were humiliated and chased back to Gilgal, having lost thirty-six of Israel's best men. Israel was terrified, and Joshua and the elders were discouraged. Joshua was so upset that he blamed God for the defeat, saying, "Alas, O Lord God, wherefore has thou at all brought this people over Jordan, to deliver us into the hand of the Amorites, to destroy us? would to God we had been content, and dwelt on the other side of Jordan!" (Joshua 7:7).

The problem with Israel's attack on Ai was not tactical, but spiritual. The loss in Ai wasn't even about Ai. Israel failed because of unresolved sin committed during the attack on Jericho. Joshua had failed to make sure Israel obeyed God's instructions concerning Jericho. After one day of fighting, with Jericho in ruins, Joshua was now ready to withdraw from the region and quit fighting because Ai had whipped them. He was guilty of the sin of unbelief.

Q: Have you ever felt like giving up because you failed, maybe
made the same mistake or committed the same sin you've
done before?

A: _____

_____

Q: According to 1 John 1:8 and 10, do you think God knows that
you have sinned?

A: _____

_____

Q: According to 1 John 1:9, what should you do about it?

A: _____

_____

Q: If you do what 1 John 1:9 says to do, what has God promised to
do?

A: _____

_____

When faced with problems, aren't you often tempted to despair? It
will help if you'll remember that you don't have all the information.
Only God knows everything. All is not lost. You may be "cast down,"
but you are "not destroyed" (2 Corinthians 4:9). We need to learn
that not every difficulty is a defeat. However, like Joshua, we also
need to realize that real defeat comes as the result of sin in some
area of life. You've not necessarily been defeated when things don't
go your way. You've been defeated when one of the enemies of your
soul gains an advantage and you fall into sin.

Q: What kind of situation have you experienced that tempted you
to despair?

A: _____

_____

Q: How did you deal with it, or how could you have dealt with it more biblically?

A: _____

_____

While Joshua was in despair over the situation involving Ai, the real problem had been in his failure to fully obey at Jericho. In his enthusiasm over the great victory at Jericho, Joshua had missed the fact that it was tainted by sin. The judgment of God fell in a situation in which Joshua had done nothing wrong. Joshua's anguish was misdirected toward what he was going through at the moment rather than the prior sin that had caused it.

Q: What lesson can you learn from this for your own life today?

A: _____

_____

God told Joshua to find the man guilty of taking for himself that which belonged to God and remove the sin from Israel. God would help, but there would be nothing private about the way the culprit would be identified. Starting with the tribal leaders, God would narrow down the field of suspects to the very man. God knew all along who was guilty. Israel had to go through the rather harrowing process for several reasons. First, the magistrates had to learn to administer justice by God's guidance. Second, this method would help motivate everyone in Israel to examine their own hearts for sin. Third, it gave the guilty a lot of opportunity to confess. Finally, once the guilty party was identified, it eliminated any question in Israel about who he was and the genuineness of his guilt.

Achan held out to the bitter end. He admitted nothing until he was identified; then, rather than making any kind of confession to God, he merely admitted to Joshua what he had done. He had seen some of the valuable goods of Jericho and decided to keep them for himself. Knowing it was wrong, he hid them under his tent. Essentially, his sin was failure to tithe. God had promised Israel the goods of the land of Canaan. He asked only that the goods from the first city—"the first-fruits"—be set aside for Him. But Achan wanted more. Maybe he was afraid that if he gave the first part to God that he couldn't trust God to make the rest of what he would earn enough to meet his needs.

Another reason God demanded that Israel give to Him all of the goods from the very first city they conquered in Canaan was to teach them that future victory would depend on present obedience, particularly in the matter of tithing.

Q: Do you think other victories for you might depend on your obedience to this principle?

A: _____

_____

Q: Are you willing to obey God in this matter?

A: _____

_____

Q: What do you think might be the consequences of disobedience?

A: _____

_____

Q: What do you think might be some of the blessings of obedience?

A: _____

_____

We can learn several things from Achan's bad example. First, we see that the principle of the tithe is important to God, and failure to tithe is serious. It combines covetousness—dissatisfaction with what God has given us—with blasphemy and idolatry—keeping for ourselves what belongs to God.

Q: How do you think keeping for yourself something that belongs to God might demonstrate the following sins?

Unbelief _____

_____

Pride _____

_____

Idolatry _____

_____

We also learn that trying to hide our sin from God is pointless. Further, we see that God hates sin in His own people as much as He hates sin in those who are not His. Even the best of us are capable of great sin, and our sin has the potential of causing great harm to others. "Let him that thinketh he standeth take heed lest he fall" (1 Corinthians 10:12).

PROJECTS FOR DEVELOPING AN OBEDIENT FAITH

1. List a few circumstances that have brought difficulties into your life. Identify which ones were defeats, caused by sin, and which were difficulties sent to teach or strengthen you. What are some lessons you have learned from these circumstances?

_____

_____

_____

_____

_____

_____

_____

_____

2. Think about your situation in life as a child in your family or as a member of your class or other peer group. Are there sinful situations you need to address in your life or the life of another person? Begin to pray for wisdom and courage to deal properly with the situations you are facing or may face in the future and commit yourself to honoring God with your life. Start writing out a strategy for addressing the situations, including seeking any help or counsel you might need from a pastor, parent, or teacher.

_____

_____

_____

_____

_____

_____

_____

_____

_____

_____

_____

_____

_____

_____

_____

Lesson 8
"What If I Blow It?"

*Sin in your life must be dealt with honestly and
thoroughly, but once it has been resolved you have
to get on with the business of serving God.*

Memory Verse: Hebrews 8:12 "I will be merciful to their unrighteousness, and their sins and their iniquities will I remember no more."

Bible Reading: Joshua 8:1–35

Israel had blown it. After their great victory over Jericho, they had turned around and been defeated—actually, humiliated—at Ai. Thirty-six good men had died because of the sin of Achan, a man they had trusted. Even worse, God's reputation had been tarnished, and His enemies had been encouraged. No wonder Joshua and the nation of Israel were so discouraged. They were wondering if God would ever bless them again.

Q: Have you ever experienced a time of such deep sorrow for your sin that you felt dirty, defiled, useless, and unforgiveable?

A: _____

_____

If you haven't, maybe you've never admitted just how hideous God considers sin. In times like that you may confess your sin to God, beg His forgiveness, and still feel mired in shame and despair. You wish you could hear the voice of the Lord saying, "Fear not, neither be thou dismayed," but you hear only silence. That is one reason why studying, memorizing, and meditating on the Scriptures is so important. You need to be reminded from God's Word the promises He has already made to you.

Q: What does Jesus say in Matthew 28:20?

A: _____

_____

Q: What does God promise in Hebrews 13:5?

A: _____

_____

Q: What does John tell us in 1 John 1:9?

A: _____

_____

Satan wants to keep you wallowing in discouragement and despair. God wants to pick you up and get you going again in His service.

In Joshua 8, Israel was genuinely grieving over the way the nation had failed God and brought reproach on His name. Confession had been made—Joshua and Israel acknowledged that their defeat in Ai had been their own fault. Repentance had been demonstrated—Joshua and Israel had obediently rooted out the sin and removed it. Restitution had been paid—the stolen goods, with the remainder of Achan's property, were dedicated to God and treated according to God's instructions. God forgave Israel's sin.

In the midst of their mourning, God spoke words of encouragement to Joshua. Genuine sorrow was important, but Israel must not be overcome with grief to the point of despair. They needed to be confident of God's forgiveness. He was still their God; they were still His people. Canaan was still God's gift to Israel; they must still fight to conquer and control the land.

Because they had dealt thoroughly with their sin, Israel's relationship with God was mended. However, their reputation in the eyes of the Canaanites needed improvement. The little band from Ai had put them to open shame. God promised them victory over Ai this time, so they could move against the city with confidence, but they actually had to go. This illustrates the principle that God's promises are never to be used as an excuse for laziness, but as an encouragement to diligent, hard-working obedience.

Just as we are to make no compromise with sin, Israel was ordered to show no mercy to the inhabitants of Ai, the same as in Jericho. The difference this time is that Israel was to salvage the goods from Ai to keep for themselves before the city was burned. God had intended the destruction of the goods of Jericho to illustrate the principle of the tithe—the first-fruits belong to God (Exodus 23:19a). God intended the salvaging of the goods from Ai to illustrate the principle that God rewards faithfulness—He provides for those who trust Him. Of course, 530,000 soldiers and their families were not going to get rich by taking the goods from Ai, a city of about twelve thousand people. There is no biblical justification for claiming that if you give twenty dollars to the Lord today, He will give back twenty dollars or even fifty dollars next week. What the Bible actually teaches is that if you'll honor God by giving generously to His work, He will take care of you (Philippians 4:16–19).

The spoiling of Ai proved just how foolish Achan had been. If only he'd waited! His covetousness had caused him to take for himself something God would have gladly given him in His own time.

Q: How could you apply this principle in your own life?

A: _____

_____

It's hard to imagine a greater contrast between the strategies God laid out for taking Jericho and what He said Joshua must do to take Ai. The means of taking Jericho had been bold and majestic, marching in silent confidence that God would give them the city. To take Ai, Joshua had to prepare an ambush, and he had to work out the details on his own. Apparently, God wanted Joshua and all Israel to learn humility. An ambush is usually the strategy of either a grossly inferior force or of a coward. It implied that Israel's 530,000 soldiers had to hide in the hills, sneak up on the enemy, and launch a surprise attack from behind to defeat just three thousand Canaanites. Having to turn tail and run from their enemy to draw them into a trap where others could attack would be an embarrassing admission of their own cowardice. It would make Israel in general and Joshua in particular look foolish to the people of the land. To be restored to a place of honor and respect, Joshua had to suffer humiliation.

There is an important lesson here for all of us. We must be prepared to do whatever is necessary to be right with God, even if it means humiliation. Anyone who isn't willing to do a little necessary groveling when he's been wrong is allowing his pride to keep him from being restored to fellowship with God. The genuinely repentant heart of even the greatest among us gladly says, "I abhor myself, and repent in dust and ashes" (Job 42:6). You and I must be willing to offer abject apology and beg forgiveness when we've sinned against someone.

Q: Do you find it difficult to apologize and ask forgiveness when you've sinned against someone?

A: _____

_____

Q: What do you need to do in situations like that?

A: _____

_____

Joshua organized his army and prepared the ambush. Two nights before the trap would be sprung, thirty thousand soldiers had been sent to hide behind the city, ready to plunder and burn the city when Ai's army had been enticed into battle. On the following day another five thousand were sent to the west of the city to cut off any escape in that direction. The remaining 495,000 soldiers pitched their camp on the hills facing Ai. On the night before the battle, Joshua went alone into the valley between Ai and the camp of Israel's army. At dawn, the men of Ai saw an opportunity to capture Joshua. When they rushed out into the valley, Joshua and Israel's army fled. After leading the unwary army of Ai a short distance, Joshua and his army turned to attack. Too late, the men of Ai realized their mistake. Their city was burned, and they were annihilated.

A secondary lesson from the ambush of Ai is seen in some similarities between the way the battle developed and the way sin can work. Temptation will bait you into thinking you are invincible, get your attention, lead you away from safety, then turn on you and destroy you.

Q: Briefly describe a situation in your own life or the life of someone you know that followed this pattern.

A: _____

_____

Q: What are some ways to protect yourself from such a situation in the future?

A: _____

_____

You probably have particular sins that you find especially tempting. That is implied in the fact that one is "drawn away of *his own* lust" (James 1:14). If, however, you believe you are bound by a besetting sin over which victory is impossible, you should read Romans 6 and think about what it means to be "dead to sin" and to be "more than conquerors." The enemy will surely continue to attack you at your point of greatest weakness, but God wants you to remember that He has provided the necessary power to defeat any temptation that confronts you (1 Corinthians 10:13).

Q: What particular sins do you find the most difficult to resist?

A: _____

_____

Q: What should you do the next time you are tempted to indulge in one of those sins?

A: _____

_____

We need to treat personal sin just as thoroughly and ruthlessly as Israel had to treat Achan and Ai. We must not be too proud to accept the humiliation we brought on ourselves by our disobedience and willfulness. There is no room for pride in genuine repentance. You and I should be willing to offer abject apology and beg God's forgiveness when we've sinned. If we've sinned against someone else, we need to ask his or her forgiveness too. Then when we've confessed our sin and have been forgiven and restored, we need to get on with the business of serving God.

Once they had dealt with the sin of Achan, God had assigned Israel a disciplinary program designed to prove their faith in God—an ambush of Ai. After winning that battle, they were expected to prove they still wanted to participate in the covenant God had made with Israel at Mount Sinai. Only after that was finished would they be restored to full fellowship with God and be ready for the successful conquest of Canaan.

After the total destruction of Ai, Joshua took all the people of Israel nearly fifty miles into Canaan to the twin mountains of Ebal and Gerizim. Guided by the instructions given in Deuteronomy 11:29 and 31:11–12, Joshua built an altar on Mount Ebal and wrote on its sides the words of the law. Then he offered a sacrifice on that altar to remove the curse of sin, providing for us a picture of Christ, Who bore the curse of sin for us. Because of our sin, we are justly condemned by the Law. If you've confessed your sin and trusted Christ alone to save you, the curse of the Law no longer applies to you. Believers still have to live obediently in service to our Savior, but nothing we do can enhance or detract from our acceptance in Christ. God has "made us accepted in the beloved" (Ephesians 1:6).

We've all blown it at some time or other, and because we are still human we may blow it again later. Dealing with sin in your life or confronting it in someone else is never fun. The process of confrontation, confession, restitution, and restoration can be emotionally grueling. It can also be immensely rewarding when the people involved behave with the right spirit. On the basis of Jesus' perfect righteousness and His death in our place, God is willing to forgive any sins you have committed. That is not permission to go on sinning, but grace and power to live for Him. God wants to pick you up, dust you off, and set you on your feet again so you can go on and serve Him.

PROJECT FOR DEVELOPING AN OBEDIENT FAITH

Is there someone you have wronged but before whom you have been unwilling to humble yourself and beg forgiveness? Begin to pray diligently for the character and courage to go to that person in genuine humility, offering any restitution possible and seeking to be restored to fellowship with him or her. Then do it.

Important note: Do this only for sins that are known or should be known. If the sin is one of your heart, like secret hatred or resentment, beg *God's* forgiveness, change your attitude, and leave the other person in blissful ignorance. Telling him of such things will hurt him and will not help you.

Lesson 9
When You Feel Like a Failure

When you mess things up, if you really want to honor
God He can use even your stupid choices for His glory.

Memory Verse: 1 John 1:8–9 "If we say that we have no sin, we deceive
ourselves, and the truth is not in us. If we confess our
sins, he is faithful and just to forgive us our sins, and
to cleanse us from all unrighteousness."

Bible Reading: Joshua 9:1–27

The Devil tries to defeat the believer in a lot of different ways.
Sometimes he organizes outside forces to hammer the believer for
doing right. Other times he presents enticements to tempt the believer to compromise with evil. The Canaanite responses to Joshua's
early victories were of both types.

Israel's destruction of Jericho and Ai got the attention of all the
Canaanites throughout the region. There was no central govern-
ment in Canaan, so the various cities were more or less independent
of each other. While each city had its own king, the cities of a given
region often worked together for their mutual defense. In response
to the Israelite invasion, most of the Canaanite leaders banded together to form a coalition army to drive the Israelites back across
the Jordan.

The leaders of the Gibeonites, however, were less optimistic about
their ability to defend themselves from Israel and their God. They
thought it would be smarter—and safer—to form an alliance with

Israel. As the story develops in the next few lessons, you'll see that Joshua was well prepared for the frontal assault of the united armies of the Canaanites. However, at this point he was less than fully alert to the potential danger of a subtle alliance with those God had told him to destroy.

Joshua and Israel had been on an emotional roller coaster. They had won a great victory at Jericho. Then, because of one overlooked failing, they were humiliated at Ai. Once they removed the sin and humbled themselves before God and the Canaanites, God gave them another victory over Ai. Then they had rededicated themselves to God and returned to the camp at Gilgal. They were now in the right place, doing the right thing, and in a right relationship with God. What could go wrong?

Q: Have you ever been in a situation like this: in the right place, doing the right thing, in a right relationship with God, then you did something stupid? If so, describe it briefly.

A: _____

_____

Q: Explain the significance of Paul's warning in 1 Corinthians 10:12.

A: _____

_____

The city of Gibeon was only twenty miles west of the Israelite camp at Gilgal, and only five or six miles southwest of Ai. If Israel's army kept moving in the same general direction, Gibeon was the next fortified city they would encounter. The Gibeonites had reason to believe that their destruction was sure, so they concocted a bold plan to deceive Joshua into making an alliance with them. Disguised as a weary band of travelers, representatives of Gibeon went to Gilgal to speak with Joshua. Presenting themselves as emissaries from "a very far country" (Joshua 9:9), they came asking for peace.

At first Joshua was suspicious. He challenged them as potential enemies. When the Gibeonites lied and assured him they were from far away, Joshua had their baggage inspected. Finding their provisions stale, moldy, and beat up, and their clothes nearly worn out, Joshua decided to believe them.

Q: In what way do you think the Gibeonites' claim to have come from a far country to ask for peace might have appealed to Joshua's pride?

A: _____

_____

Q: What are some things young men may be tempted to do because they think it would make them more popular?

A: _____

_____

Even great men of God are not immune to the seduction of popularity and fame. But the real dilemma for Joshua was in sorting out his obligations. Joshua had been given two sets of instructions in Deuteronomy 20:10–17.

Q: What was Joshua to do to the people of the land of Canaan, including the tribe of the Hivites to which the Gibeonites belonged (Deuteronomy 20:16–17)?

A: _____

_____

Q: What was Joshua to do in the case of any distant city with which they had conflict (Deuteronomy 20:10–15)?

A: _____

_____

Proving that he was at heart a peaceful and merciful man, Joshua accepted their story. He and the elders of Israel decided to swear a solemn oath to the Gibeonites that they would let them live. The Gibeonites could go home in peace, confident that Israel would not destroy them. Joshua's mistake was that he didn't do enough to make sure the Gibeonites' story was true.

Q: What does the Bible say Joshua did wrong (Joshua 9:14)?

A: _____

_____

It may seem that Joshua had an advantage over us in that he could expect God to talk to him directly to give him instructions. However, he had been told to study "this book of the law" (Joshua 1:8) in order to know what to do. Joshua had only the first five books of the Bible to guide him. We have all sixty-six books of inspired Scripture to guide us, so the advantage is really ours.

Q: According to 2 Timothy 3:16–17, why do you think we have an advantage over Joshua in knowing what God wants us to do?

A: _____

_____

For you and me to avoid compromise with sin, we need careful, constant self-examination in the light of Scripture. We need the guidance of God's Word and the conviction of His Spirit to avoid falling into sin. We can't trust our senses, because sin can be so attractive. The truth is no believer would ever fall prey to temptation if it were presented as it really is from God's perspective.

Sometimes we make mistakes, even when we want to do the right thing. It wasn't long—just three days—before Joshua discovered they'd been duped. Joshua had a serious problem. If he keeps his vow to spare the Gibeonites, he deliberately disobeys God's instructions to destroy all the inhabitants of the land. But if he breaks his promise because the Gibeonites lied, he deliberately violates his own solemn oath sworn in the presence of God and in God's name.

Joshua and the elders of Israel decided wisely. They would demonstrate proper reverence for God's name and take their lumps for having made a foolish promise. They would not try to get out of trouble for disobeying God by blaspheming God's name by breaking their vow.

What if you promised some friends that you would do something sinful with them or for them? Should you keep that promise? No. You should tell them that you can't do it, because it is wrong. You have a higher obligation to honor God. Such a situation is not the same as the one facing Joshua. Joshua was trying to follow God's instructions and made a solemn vow before God. While it was much more important, it was more like signing a contract to buy a car and make monthly payments. Even if you later find out that it was a dumb decision, you still have to make the payments.

Q: How do you think this principle would apply in the case of making a vow of marriage to keep yourself "only unto her, for better or for worse, for richer or poorer, in sickness and in health, to love, honor, and to cherish, till death do you part, so help me God"?

A: _____

_____

_____

Q: What if later you discovered that the girl you married wasn't saved, and you know God wanted you to marry only a believer? On the basis of this principle and what Jesus says in Mark 10:4–12, what should you do?

A: _____

_____

_____

Q: List at least five important decisions you are facing now or will have to make in the future, and start praying today for the wisdom to make the right choices:

1. _____

2. _____

3. _____

4. _____

5. _____

When Joshua found out that the Gibeonites had lied to him, he mustered Israel to march to Gibeon to confront those who had deceived them. When they got there, Joshua announced that Israel would keep their word, but that for their deception the Gibeonites would be "cursed." This did not mean that evil would come upon them, but that they were set apart to God (see Joshua 6:18 and 7:1). The Gibeonites responded by confessing their guilt and their fear of God, and by willingly submitting to His authority. As a result, they weren't just spared. They were blessed in the service of worship. They would be "hewers of wood and drawers of water for the house of my God" (Joshua 9:23). While their position was a lowly one, they were accepted into Israel as full participants in their society and inducted into God's covenant with Israel (Deuteronomy 20:10–15).

Once again, we see God being merciful to people who don't deserve it. Just as in the case of Rahab, or in your own case for that matter, God blessed the Gibeonites because they confessed their sin and turned to God in faith.

How do you think Joshua felt? I'm sure he felt like a failure. He hadn't asked God for instructions and had made an alliance God had forbidden. The fact that it turned out for good was in spite of Joshua's disobedience, not because of it. It is important to note, though, that Joshua wasn't trying to disobey God; he was trying to do the right thing. He wanted to honor God, but he was distracted. He got careless and messed up. This incident proves that even when we mess things up, if we truly want to honor God, He can use our errors in judgment for His glory.

Q: Can you think of a time when you were trying to do the right thing but got careless and ended up doing something wrong?

A: _____

_____

_____

Q: Have you confessed your carelessness to God and asked Him to help you make things right?

A: _____

_____

_____

Q: What have you learned from the experience?

A: _____

_____

_____

Q: What do you think Romans 8:28 means in regard to this discussion?

A: _____

_____

_____

Q: What does the Bible say you should do when you are faced with making a decision without having any definite way of proving that one choice or another is the right one (Proverbs 3:5–6; James 1:5)?

A: _____

_____

_____

G. Campbell Morgan was a great preacher from the last century. He once said, "A false step taken by a Christian can be forgiven by God. But you must live with the consequences the rest of your life." Does that mean that you are doomed to live in constant fear of making a wrong choice? No! If your choices are made on the basis of your study of Scripture, careful evaluation of your options, and prayer, with a genuine desire to honor God, you are not capable of making serious mistakes. You cannot derail God's program. You are secure in His care.

PROJECTS FOR DEVELOPING AN OBEDIENT FAITH

1. Obviously, honoring your word is pretty important to God. Do you consistently tell the truth and honor your word? If not, what are some lies or broken promises that you need to make right?

_____

_____

_____

_____

_____

_____

_____

2. Do you find yourself having to live with the consequences of one or more wrong choices? Have you taken them to God for forgiveness? Have you done what you can to make things right with others affected by those choices? Then pray for the wisdom to make the best of your situation and for the faith to trust a great and gracious God to bring glory to Himself through your life.

_____

_____

_____

_____

_____

_____

_____

_____

Lesson 10
When Life Seems Too Hard to Take

*When you are not strong enough for the challenges you
face, you can rely on your Savior. The enemy may be
strong, and the day may be long, but the victory is sure!*

Memory Verse: 2 Corinthians 12:9–10 "And he said unto me, My
grace is sufficient for thee: for my strength is made
perfect in weakness. Most gladly therefore will I
rather glory in my infirmities, that the power of
Christ may rest upon me. Therefore I take pleasure
in infirmities, in reproaches, in necessities, in perse-
cutions, in distresses for Christ's sake: for when I am
weak, then am I strong."

Bible Reading: Joshua 10:1–27 and 11:1–15

What is the closing line of every fairy tale you have ever read? "And
they lived happily ever after." Having overcome some great difficulty,
maybe even involving supernatural forces working against them, the
heroes of the story move on and never have another problem. That
is why they call them "fairy tales." Most of them have an important
moral to teach, but they don't fully correspond with reality.

Many believers have a "fairy tale" view of Christianity. They think
that accepting the Lord Jesus means that they should have no more
troubles. Unfortunately, that is precisely what many preachers have
told them. The problem is that when they are faced with a real crisis,
their faith can be shaken.

You shouldn't be surprised that life is tough. Jesus predicted that the gates of hell would storm His church, but would not prevail against her (Matthew 16:18). Satan will do everything he can to trip you up, discourage you, or defeat you until you reach heaven, but God has given you the resources you need to be victorious.

In Joshua 9:1–2 we read that all the people of Canaan had decided to form an alliance to defeat Israel. This coalition of Amorites included the Hivites, a group to which the Gibeonites belonged. The other Hivites of that region were not happy to hear that the Gibeonites had made peace with Israel. They saw their defection to Israel as betrayal. Because the city of Gibeon was known to be powerful, the other Canaanites in the area were not just angry. They were terrified. Five kings from southern Canaan decided to postpone their plans to attack Israel and joined their forces together to deal with Gibeon. When this southern coalition moved out, the Gibeonites did not play the hypocrite. They didn't try to appease their old friends and relatives by claiming to still be on the side of the Amorites. Instead, they sent Joshua an urgent plea for help.

Q: Can other people tell by your actions that you are loyal to Christ?

A: _____

_____

Q: Are you sometimes tempted to pretend not to be a Christian so your friends or family won't give you a hard time?

A: _____

_____

Q: What are some things you could or should change about the way you think, talk, and act that would help prove your loyalty to Christ?

A: _____

_____

Becoming a Christian is more than just joining a church or reciting a prayer. Genuine conversion involves a radical change of loyalties. Once you come to Christ, there is a new King in charge of your life—the Lord Jesus. You may not follow your new King perfectly, but you've pledged your loyalty to a new Sovereign. Many new Christians find that their family and friends turn against them. Like the Gibeonites, you have help that you can call on in your distress. When you feel too weak for the dangers you face, you can rely on your Savior. His "grace is sufficient" for you, and His "strength is made perfect" in your weakness.

Q: Have you had members of your family or old friends turn on you because of your loyalty to Christ?

A: _____

_____

Q: If so, what happened? If not, why do you think that is?

A: _____

_____

Q: When the Gibeonites were attacked by their family and old friends for having joined Israel, how did the Gibeonites respond (Joshua 10:6)?

A: _____

_____

Q: If something similar happens to you, what should you do for help (Romans 10:13)?

A: _____

_____

It would have been easy for Joshua to find reasons for not going to the aid of the Gibeonites. He'd promised not to harm them, but he didn't exactly promise to help them. Still, Joshua's honor demanded that he keep all of the promises his word implied. He responded immediately, because his duty was clear. Taking his army nearly thirty miles through rugged terrain while climbing over three thousand feet, they marched through the night to arrive early the next morning. When they arrived, God encouraged Joshua with a promise of victory (Joshua 10:8).

Q: Have you ever thought, "God would never bother to help me; I've been too bad"?

A: _____

_____

Q: When Joshua went to help the Gibeonites, was it because the Gibeonites were good, honest, and upright people, or was it because Joshua was a good, honest, and upright leader?

A: _____

_____

Q: Do you think the Lord's help for yourself depends on your being good, or does it depend on His being good?

A: _____

_____

New converts often face their greatest opposition immediately. They may be forsaken or even attacked by their old friends and family. Lacking experience or Bible training, they aren't well prepared to face the challenges of spiritual conflict alone. Mature believers must be prepared to help them.

Q: Write down some of the challenges you are facing and list the names of some mature believers you can turn to for help. If you can't think of any mature believer who might help you, start praying now for such people in your life.

A: _____

_____

Q: List some new converts you know who might need your encouragement. Begin praying for them and looking for opportunities to help them.

A: _____

_____

As Joshua brings the army of Israel to help the Gibeonites, we see
another contrast in his tactics. When Israel moved against Jericho,
they had approached deliberately, almost in slow motion. When
they conquered Ai, they had to use a carefully planned and cho-
reographed ambush. But in dealing with the armies of the southern mountain cities, Joshua launched a ferocious, headlong attack.
When the forces of Israel came charging out of the hills at dawn,
the Amorite coalition forces were caught completely by surprise. In
almost total disarray, the enemy fled. Many of the Amorite forces
fell to the swords of Israel right there at Gibeon.

The Amorites had badly miscalculated in at least three areas.
First, they didn't expect Israel to help the "strangers" (Gibeonites) in
an unbiased way, as if they were born Israelites. Second, they didn't
understand Israel's dedication to total victory over the Canaanites,
including the Amorites. Third, they didn't comprehend the awe-
some power of God and that He fought for Israel.

As the rest of the Amorites fled through a mountain pass, God
sent a storm of huge hailstones that killed more of the Amorites
than had the army of Israel, and harmed none of Israel's men. The
hailstones hit and killed thousands of the fleeing Amorites, and
none of the Israelites who were chasing them. Only God could do
that. If Joshua had any lingering doubts about whether or not God
wanted him to keep his promise to the Gibeonites, the hailstorm
put his mind at ease.

Q: In what way do you think the hailstorm might have increased
Joshua's faith?

A: _____

_____

Q: In what way do you think the hailstorm might have increased the faith and confidence of the Gibeonites?

A: _____

_____

God's blessing on Israel that day was so obvious to Joshua that he decided to make an incredibly daring request. He asked God to stop the movement of the sun and moon—to suspend time itself—in order to give the army of Israel enough daylight to complete the destruction of the Amorites. The nature of the request implies that Joshua was also asking God for the army to have the strength to keep fighting. Remember, they had marched thirty miles uphill all night and had been chasing the enemy through the mountains all morning. The most amazing thing about Joshua's request is that God did what he asked! God proved again that He controls the universe, as Paul explains that by Him "all things consist (hold together)" (Colossians 1:17).

Q: How might Deuteronomy 33:25b–26 have encouraged Joshua to make such an audacious request as to ask the sun to stand still?

A: _____

_____

Q: The deadly hailstorm and the miraculously lengthened day had a profound effect on the rest of the Canaanites of the region. Their response is summarized in the last half of Joshua 10:21. Explain their reaction in your own words.

A: _____

_____

We see again that victory depended on the obedient faith of Joshua and Israel. They had to go fight, but the battle was won by God's help, not military skill. Still, Joshua and Israel were about to learn another important lesson. Their great victory over the southern coalition had been exciting and encouraging, but they were not going to be able to relax. Even tougher challenges lay ahead. Soon, the much more powerful kings of northern Canaan heard that their southern allies had been defeated. They gathered their armies near Merom, about eighty miles north of Gilgal. This force included a host of armored chariots. For the first time, Israel would be facing an army that possessed far better weapons and was at least as large as their own.

So, naturally, God told Joshua to attack. He also told Joshua to destroy the chariots and horses, not to confiscate them. God did not want the Canaanites to fear Israel's army; He wanted them to fear Him. Joshua's destruction of the horses and chariots would prove he didn't need the methods of the world to be victorious—he needed the Lord.

Q: Can you think of any way to apply that lesson in your own life?

A: _____

_____

Joshua 11 summarizes a military campaign that lasted at least five and maybe seven years. The passage provides a record of Joshua's complete obedience (Joshua 11:15) and tells us of the eventual ending of hostilities (Joshua 11:23) as the Canaanites were completely defeated. This foreshadows the final rest that will come when evil is removed from the world once and for all when Christ comes back to reign forever as King of kings and Lord of lords (Hebrews 4:8–11; Revelation 11:15; 19:16).

From Joshua's great campaign of Canaanite conquest we learn that entering Canaan is not a picture of life in heaven but of life in Christ. There are enemies to confront and conquer, and we must be constantly on our guard. We also learn that the battles we face must actually be fought and won. The spiritual enemies of our souls may not be visible, but they are real (Ephesians 6:12). We must not become lazy and give up the fight, for we know that our labor is not in vain in the Lord (1 Corinthians 15:58). Finally, we learn that to be victorious, we have to obey.

Do we ever get to rest? Yes. God gives us present "rest" from frustration, discouragement, and fear. To enjoy that rest we must have absolute confidence in Christ alone to give us victory. But we must also "labor . . . to enter into that rest" (Hebrews 4:11). That is, we have to make entering that rest something for which we diligently strive. Like Joshua, we must do everything Christ tells us to do. God promises a permanent and perfect rest from sin and the curse. This is a rest we will enjoy only partially in this life, but fully in the resurrection when "this corruptible shall have put on incorruption" (1 Corinthians 15:54).

The Lord has promised you, as a believer in Christ Jesus, the spiritual stamina to keep fighting to the end. "Being confident of this very thing, that he which hath begun a good work in you will perform it until the day of Jesus Christ" (Philippians 1:6; see also Romans 8:16–18). Your confidence is not in *who* you are, but in *Whose* you are. No obstacle we face can "separate us from the love of God, which is in Christ Jesus our Lord" (Romans 8:39). It is when we get to heaven that we will live "happily ever after." In the meantime, the enemy may be strong and the day may be long, but the victory is sure!

PROJECT FOR DEVELOPING AN OBEDIENT FAITH

Read Philippians 1:6 and Romans 8:16–39. In the light of those passages, explain the statement, "The day may be long and the enemy may be strong, but the victory is sure."

_____

_____

_____

_____

_____

_____

_____

Lesson 11
When Is Enough, Enough?

You must always be contented with what God is doing in your life, but you must never stop trying to grow spiritually.

Memory Verse: Philippians 3:13–14 "Brethren, I count not myself to have apprehended: but this one thing I do, forgetting those things which are behind, and reaching forth unto those things which are before, I press toward the mark for the prize of the high calling of God in Christ Jesus"

Bible Reading: Joshua 13:1–6; 17:14–18; 18:2–10; 19:9, 47

For several years, my wife taught first graders in a Christian day school. The annual Christmas party was one of the highlights of the year for the students. Although it's probably for the wrong reasons, children tend to love Christmas. Eagerly counting down the days, they can hardly wait for the gifts they expect to receive. Usually my wife had each student bring an inexpensive gift, already wrapped, for the student gift exchange. Boys brought gifts boys would like, and girls brought "girly" gifts. On the day of the party, the gifts would be numbered, and the children would draw numbers to see which gift they would receive. All the children were excited, expecting to find some great treasure under the gift wrap. Typically, some would still be pleased after they opened their gifts, but many would be disappointed. Often, a lot of trading went on after the gifts were unwrapped as the kids made deals with one another to swap for something they wanted more than the gifts they had received.

Even in something as simple as a children's gift exchange, we see evidence of our fallen human nature. We tend to want more than we get, so we are often disappointed. Covetousness is not learned; it's natural. Contentment must be learned and is supernatural. The next section of Joshua describes the distribution of gifts far more valuable than toys in a gift exchange. Joshua was giving out parcels of land. It would be allotted by drawing, and trading was forbidden. Whatever you get, you keep. The potential for conflict was enormous.

Q: *Covetousness* means "longing for more than God has given you, or longing for something other than what God has given you." *Contentment* means "being satisfied with what God has given you." Describe a situation in which you displayed one or the other.

A: _____

_____

By this time, Joshua was nearly ninety years old, but God told him there was more to do. Even though Israel had conquered the Canaanites, they had not yet actually taken possession of everything God had given them. There was still "very much land to be possessed" (Joshua 13:1). Israel controlled Canaan, but the Canaanite enemies that remained were still dangerous. Israel must not become complacent and let down their guard. That is essentially the warning that Paul sounds for believers today in the memory verse for this lesson, Philippians 3:13–14. Paul is not talking about working toward a higher position in Christ, because every believer is already exalted by being "in Christ" (1 Corinthians 1:30–31; Galatians 3:26–28; Ephesians 1:3). The "high calling" Paul refers to is the "upward call" or "heavenly call" of God. Paul means that rather than drifting through life on the memories of past victories, we have to keep fighting the Enemy until the Lord calls us home to heaven.

Q: What are some "enemies" (temptations, sins, adversaries) with which you are still struggling?

A: _____

_____

Q: What do you think you could do to keep your guard up and not be defeated by them?

A: _____

_____

It is amazing that the account of the land distribution records no evidence of disputation over property rights, preferences, or procedures. The people willingly set aside personal desires and submitted to the will of the Lord in assigning them particular territories. The land assignments were permanent and perpetual—Israel's law did not allow for the sale of land. All of the land given out by the Lord through Joshua was to remain the territory of the tribe to which it was assigned.

Q: How did Israel's acceptance of land assignment by casting lots demonstrate mature faith?

A: _____

_____

Why does Joshua include such a detailed account of the land assignments? The obvious reason was to provide a written record for future generations describing which portion was assigned to which people. More importantly, it was to emphasize that the land was God's gift to Israel. They had conquered the land because God fought for them. Now individual tribes and families would settle specific parcels of land because God gave it to them. To be victorious, they had to obey; but actual possession was all of grace. This provides another illustration of the spiritual theme of Joshua: spiritual growth requires effort and attention. We must surrender to God's will, in total submission to Him, as Israel did in casting lots for the land. We must also actually take what the Lord has given us, claiming as our own what God has provided.

Sadly, the record shows that while most of the Canaanites were destroyed by Israel, some were put under tribute (Joshua 15:63; 16:9–10; 17:12). Israel had worked hard, fought long, and made a lot of progress toward full obedience; but they did not obey completely. They apparently thought it would be wasteful to destroy the enemies who could provide cheap labor or pay a lot of taxes, so many were enslaved or charged tribute. Israel reasoned that it would be OK to disobey God as long as they came out ahead financially. We would all do well to remember their failure and not commit the same sin of compromising biblical principles for money.

Q: What are some things that you or others your age have been tempted to do wrong in order to come out ahead (more money, better grades, better performance in sports, etc.)?

A: _____

_____

Q: Read Galatians 5:19–21. What are some "works of the flesh" that you recognize in your own life or experience?

A: _____

_____

Q: Read Galatians 5:22–23. How are you doing on displaying the "fruit of the Spirit" in your life?

A: _____

_____

Q: Would you say that you still have "more territory to possess"?

A: _____

_____

While I said that there was no disputation about the land assignments, there were two tribes who complained that they did not get enough. Both Ephraim and Manasseh thought they each deserved more than "one lot and one portion" because they were so "great" or "numerous" (Joshua 17:14). Numbers 26 provides a census taken less than ten years previously. It shows that Manasseh ranked as only the sixth largest of the twelve tribes, and the only tribe smaller than Ephraim was Simeon. Furthermore, Judah was the only tribe to be allotted as much territory as these two tribes each received, and Simeon's allotment ended up being carved out of the land given to Judah (Joshua 19:9).

Q: How do you think the claim of Ephraim and Manasseh reveals the sins of pride and covetousness?

A: _____

_____

With a very gracious answer, Joshua told them that while he could not take land from the other tribes to expand theirs, there were unassigned territories that bordered their land that were still unconquered. If they needed more land, they could take it from its inhabitants. Ironically, Ephraim and Manasseh then began to complain that they couldn't do that because they were too weak. Responding with words that were both a rebuke and an encouragement, Joshua said, "You are a great people, and are very strong." He assured them that they would be able to take what they needed. He didn't say it would be easy. He just said to do it (Joshua 17:17–18).

While the essence of contentment is being satisfied with what God has given you, there is a fine line between contentment and complacency. Joshua's answer to Ephraim and Manasseh illustrates the necessary balance: be contented with what you have been given, and trust God to give you the ability to get and keep what you need. That attitude encourages both constant effort and satisfaction with the outcome. As stated in the theme of this lesson, you must always be contented with what God is doing in your life, but you must never stop trying to grow spiritually.

Seven of the tribes, however, had not taken the initiative to even be assigned a territory, content to stay in the safety of the camp at Gilgal. This was also wrong. Joshua rebuked them, made them survey the remaining land, assigned it to the tribes, and told them to go take it (Joshua 18:2–10). Perhaps learning from Joshua's reply to Ephraim and Manasseh, Judah and Dan finally demonstrated some initiative. Judah found that the territory assigned to them was more than they needed, so they had a portion of their land reassigned to Simeon (Joshua 19:9). Dan found that their territory was insufficient, so they went out and conquered an unassigned section (Joshua 19:47).

Many Christians are like Ephraim and Manasseh—discontented with their "lot" in life. Others are like the unsettled tribes, who would rather stay in camp than venture out into new territory where there are challenges to overcome. Joshua has taught a balance between contentment and complacency.

Q: People are often dissatisfied with what God has given them. What are some things for which people may envy others?

A: _____

_____

Q: People are often spiritually complacent, satisfied with their present level of growth. What are some things people should strive to improve or expand in their spiritual lives?

A: _____

_____

Q: What are some things you know you should do to grow spiritually, but you find it easy to "forget" or make excuses for not doing them?

A: _____

_____

Q: What do you believe God sees as some of your strengths and weaknesses?

A: Strengths: _____

_____

Weaknesses: _____

_____

Joshua provides an important personal example. Even though he was the leader of all Israel, he waited until last to receive an inheritance. (Levi still has to be assigned cities, but that can't be done until the other tribes subdue their territory.) His humility reminds us of the selflessness of Jesus Christ. He was contented to accept the responsibility placed on Him by the Father, set aside the glories of heaven, and become a man. He was not complacent, simply living here on earth. He went to the cross to die for you and me (Philippians 2:3–8), then conquered death and rose again so we can have eternal life. If He could leave so much, accept so little, and accomplish so much, what right do we have for laziness or complaining?

PROJECTS FOR DEVELOPING AN OBEDIENT FAITH

1. Describe some specific things in your own attitudes, actions, and relationships that you should change in order to better demonstrate the righteousness of Christ.

_____

_____

_____

_____

_____

_____

_____

2. In Joshua 14:6–15, a portion of the text not assigned for this lesson, Caleb, who represented the tribe of Judah, reminds Joshua that Moses promised to give him the land in and around the city of Hebron (Deuteronomy 1:28, 36). Casting lots was not necessary in this case, because God's will had been made clear through Moses. This illustrates that God doesn't want us to keep questioning Him about things He's already made clear. List several things that God makes clear in Scripture that we are to do or be or that we are not to do or be.

Lesson 12
Stiff Penalties and Grace

God teaches us to enforce the rules and still show mercy.

Memory Verse: Micah 6:8 "He hath shewed thee, O man, what is good; and what doth the Lord require of thee, but to do justly, and to love mercy, and to walk humbly with thy God?"

Bible Reading: Joshua 20:1–9; 22:1–31

War teaches many lessons. We've learned a lot from the war to remove Saddam Hussein from leadership in Iraq. One of the lessons has been that rebuilding a political system can be a lot more difficult than defeating an enemy army. *Removing* a regime has proven to be much easier than *replacing* one.

For Joshua and Israel, the task of setting up a nation in a newly conquered territory must have been huge. In some ways, the conquest was the easy part. Distribution and settlement of the land had a few issues but went pretty smoothly. But from that point on, administration would be a constant challenge.

After parceling out the land, Israel's next order of business was to establish a framework for enforcing civil law. The most significant law-enforcement issue would be crimes that carried a penalty of death. Under the Old Testament law, there were several such crimes. Capital offenses included murder, rape, and adultery, but they also included defiling the Sabbath and persistently disobeying your parents (and you thought a spanking or being grounded was harsh!).

Israel didn't have professional executioners whose job was taking the lives of those guilty of capital crimes. Instead, in some cases the law required the most immediate surviving victim of the crime to be the executioner. This was generally the person who brought the charges against the one who committed the crime. In the case of rape, the injured girl or her father or husband would "cast the first stone." In the case of adultery, the spouses of the ones involved were the primary executioners. In the case of a stubbornly rebellious child, the parents were responsible for carrying out the sentence. In murder cases, the victim's next-of-kin was the executioner. The person who was to act as the executioner was called "the avenger of blood."

To convict a person of murder required the testimony of at least two witnesses. They did not have to provide firsthand accounts of the crime itself, but testified to the attitude of the perpetrator toward the victim, especially as to whether he "hated him." A fugitive found guilty of taking the life of a man he hated was presumed to be guilty of intentional murder. When the connection between hatred and murder is spoken of in the New Testament (1 John 3:15), it is nothing new. It is foundational to the very definition of murder in Old Testament law. The whole idea of "murder" assumes that the victim was innocent and the killer had a selfish motive. That's why taking a life in self defense isn't murder—the "victim" isn't innocent. It's also why taking a life accidentally isn't murder—the killer didn't act selfishly. By contrast, executing a murderer isn't murder—the "victim" has been proven guilty, and the executioner's motive is justified.

Q: Briefly explain the difference between murder and the execution of a murderer.

A: _____

_____

Joshua 20:1–9 tells us about the establishing of the cities of refuge in order to handle the most difficult and important of legal cases—

those involving the loss of human life and the need to determine whether or not it had been murder. There were six widely scattered cities in Israel, three on each side of Jordan, that were designated as cities of refuge. Israel was to provide a well-marked road to each one and appoint officers to hear the cases in each city. Someone who had done something that caused another person to die could flee to any of the six cities and find temporary refuge. If he was found guilty of murder, he would be turned over to "the avenger of blood" for execution. If the death were found to have been accidental, he would be allowed to live as long as he stayed in the city to which he had fled.

Because the cities of refuge were scattered, everyone in the land was close to one of them. Because there were well-marked roads leading to each of them, anyone could find the way to a place of safety. Because the elders of each of those cities were required to accept "all the children of Israel" and "the stranger that sojourneth among them" (Gentiles, non-Jews), anyone could find help without ethnic discrimination.

Q: How do the cities of refuge provide a picture of God's accessibility?

A: _____

_____

The provision of these cities also teaches man's responsibility. Even if the death were accidental, the taking of a life was serious. In such a case, I suppose the killer had three choices. One, he could stay home, make excuses for the accident, and explain that moving to one of the cities of refuge was too much trouble. Second, he could recognize the need to flee the avenger of blood and assume that any city would do as long as he sincerely wanted protection. Either of these might sound reasonable, but both would be disastrous. The only option that would truly save the life of the manslayer was to actually go to the nearest city of refuge for shelter on God's terms, not his own, and take up permanent residence there.

One of the most important lessons to learn from the cities of refuge is to see that being sorry for sin and understanding the penalty of death is not enough to save a sinner. The only way for you to be saved is for you to flee to Christ, casting yourself upon His mercy in gratitude for the sanctuary He alone can provide. The primary lesson of the cities of refuge is this: *To be saved, you must leave everything and come to Christ* (Luke 14:26: John 10:27; 12:26).

Q: Explain in your own words why "being sorry for sin and understanding the penalty of death is not enough to save a sinner."

A: _____

_____

Q: Have you left everything to flee to Christ?

A: _____

_____

Q: What worldly things are you having trouble leaving behind as you flee to Christ?

A: _____

_____

Q: Are any of those things worth enough to you to forfeit heaven and choose hell?

A: _____

_____

Finally, it was time for Joshua to permit the soldiers from Reuben, Gad, and one half of Manasseh to return to their inheritance on the east side of Jordan. They are sometimes called "the Transjordanian tribes" because they lived on the other side of the Jordan from the rest of Israel. These tribes had promised to fight for their brethren before settling their own land, and had done so for seven long years. They served faithfully throughout the conquest and waited patiently throughout the lengthy process of surveying the land and dividing it among the other tribes.

Q: How do you think their example of faithful service and postponed reward applies to the Christian today?

A: _____

_____

Before sending them home, Joshua charged them with their spiritual obligations to God. He commanded them to love the Lord, to walk in His ways, to keep (safeguard as precious) His commandments, to cleave (cling or stick tightly) to Him, and to serve Him. This five-fold challenge is the responsibility of every believer today.

Q: Explain how you could apply the five parts of this challenge in your own life.

To love the Lord _____

_____

To walk in His ways _____

_____

To keep His commandments _____

_____

To cleave to Him _____

_____

To serve Him _____

_____

When the Transjordanian tribes reached the eastern bank of the Jordan, before returning to their families, they "built there . . . a great altar to see to" (Joshua 22:10). This caused an immediate reaction among the other tribes, who assumed that the altar was intended either as a substitute for the memorial altar on Mount Ebal or to take the place of the altar of sacrifice in the tabernacle at Shiloh. Either one would have amounted to setting up a false worship, forbidden by God. Israel was not afraid that the Transjordanian tribes would forsake the Lord for other gods, but that they would rebel against God by offering sacrifices on unapproved altars. The principle at stake is our submission to God's right to tell us how He wants to be worshiped.

Q: How do you think this principle might apply to worship in the church today?

A: _____

_____

Fearing the worst, the western tribes immediately called out the militia and assembled at Shiloh, prepared to attack the Transjordanian tribes as apostates. However, they showed some restraint by not going straight off to war. Instead, the council decided to send Phinehas, son of Eleazar the High Priest, to lead a delegation to meet with the leaders of the Transjordanian tribes.

Phinehas confronted them and explained the nation's concerns. As a solution, he made an incredibly generous offer. He said that the western tribes were willing to make room for the Transjordanian tribes on the west side of Jordan so there might be no apostasy in their tribes and no division in Israel. They were prepared to give up part of their land to make places for three other tribes within their territory.

Q: If you saw one of your friends or family members doing something you knew would displease God, what would you be willing to give up for their good?

A: _____

_____

The Transjordanian tribes were stunned, not by the offer, but by the accusation. They had no intention of turning from God or from the rest of Israel. They wanted their new monument to be a replica of the one in Gilgal, not a rival of those in Mount Ebal or Shiloh. It was to remind future generations of their children and grandchildren, and those of the western tribes, that they were one people, serving the same God. Hearing this, Phinehas rejoiced and returned to the council of elders to report that all was well. An unnecessary civil war was avoided by the wisdom of Phinehas and the council of elders.

The primary lesson of this incident is not that you should avoid doing anything that someone else might find questionable. While you should avoid doing things to provoke people on purpose, anything you do could be misinterpreted by others. The primary lesson is also not that you should be alert to the spiritual dangers faced by your brothers and sisters in Christ. While you are not to tolerate sin, neither are you to jump to conclusions or rush to judgment. You should give them the benefit of the doubt until you talk to them.

This incident does teach us how we should handle potential disagreements among us. Churches that practice such loving confrontation when discipline is necessary demonstrate real godliness. Individual believers who practice such humility when they have a conflict with someone else may find great joy in restored relationships instead of the sadness and turmoil of broken ones. Phinehas was a true "peacemaker" (Matthew 5:9). He did not avoid confrontation, but he had a heart willing to be peaceable if possible. Israel's administration in the Promised Land involved stiff penalties for disobedience, but they were always tempered by grace. God expects us to treat sin in our own lives ruthlessly—rooting it out and destroying it whenever we find it. God also expects us to treat one another with kindness and mercy—never condoning sin, but unwilling to jump to conclusions and slow to take offense.

Projects for Developing an Obedient Faith

1. In lesson three, it was suggested that you write out the story of your conversion to Christ. If you did not do so in that lesson, do so now. If you did, look it over to see if you have adequately explained salvation. If you have not yet shared this testimony with unsaved friends, family, or neighbors, start planning for opportunities to do so.

   _____

   _____

   _____

   _____

   _____

   _____

2. Phinehas's handling of the situation with the Transjordanian tribes teaches us a lot about how to deal with conflicts. Are you facing situations that you may need to deal with in the light of what you have learned from Phinehas? Are there matters you should have handled more tactfully or to which you should have responded more temperately? If so, what can you do about it?

   _____

   _____

   _____

   _____

   _____

   _____

   _____

Lesson 13
What God Expects from You

It may be easier to pray for forgiveness than to fight temptation, but God expects you to resist the enticements of the world around you and the sin nature within you, dedicating yourself to living for the Lord.

Memory Verse: Joshua 24:15 "And if it seem evil unto you to serve the Lord, choose you this day whom ye will serve; whether the gods which your fathers served that were on the other side of the flood, or the gods of the Amorites, in whose land ye dwell: but as for me and my house, we will serve the Lord."

Bible Reading: Joshua 23:1–24:33

As we come to the final lesson from the life of Joshua, we look in on him after nearly twenty years had passed since the events described in the previous lesson. Joshua was old and knew he wouldn't live much longer. Before he died, he wanted to challenge the people of Israel to apply themselves. Like a top athlete who has to keep training to continue to perform at his best, Israel had to keep obeying the Lord to continue to enjoy His blessings in Canaan. So Joshua called the leadership of Israel to gather for a council meeting. In general, the enemy had been subdued, but Joshua needed to remind the nation that they had to remain alert to danger.

The message Joshua delivered at this meeting is recorded in Joshua 23:1–16. In it, he issued four charges to Israel's leaders. First, he said that Israel must continue to rely upon God (Joshua 23:3–5). By using the names *Yahweh* ("the Lord") and *Elohim* ("God") together, Joshua reminded Israel that God's covenants with Israel were due to His grace—they had not earned them—and that God has the power to keep those covenants.

Q: What are some things God has done for you by His grace—that you don't deserve?

A: _____

_____

Q: Since you know that God has the power to keep His promises, what are some ways this knowledge can give you confidence and help you obey God?

A: _____

_____

Joshua's second challenge was for Israel to be courageous (Joshua 23:6–7). He explained that they would demonstrate their courage by obeying God in spite of opposition and temptation. What is so courageous about doing what you are told? When enemies oppose the right, and friends encourage the wrong, and even your own flesh tempts you to disobey, remaining true to God's Word may be the most courageous thing you will ever do. It can take tremendous courage to trust God and do right when temptations pound on you or life's circumstances are frightening or discouraging.

Q: Briefly describe a situation or two in which you remember needing a lot of courage to do the right thing.

A: _____

_____

Q: Can you think of a time or two when you did the wrong thing because you didn't have the courage to obey God? If so, briefly describe them.

A: _____

_____

Q: What could you, or should you do if a similar situation comes up again?

A: _____

_____

Third, Joshua charged the leaders to "cleave unto God" (Joshua 23:8–10). That is, they needed to demonstrate a single-minded dedication of heart and life to willing obedience in everything.

Q: Do you think God would describe your attitude toward Him as "cleaving unto God"? Why or why not?

A: _____

_____

Finally, Joshua reminded them that they must love God (Joshua 23:11–12). Love for God is shown both positively and negatively. The positive aspect of your love for God is seen in giving God first place in your heart, living your life to please Him. The negative aspect of loving God involves closing your heart to anything unworthy of God.

Q: What are some practical ways you could demonstrate that you have given God first place in your heart?

A: _____

_____

Q: What are some practical ways you could demonstrate that you have closed your heart to anything unworthy of God?

A: _____

_____

Joshua also explained why Israel should remain faithful. He warned them that the presence of many of the Canaanites still living among them could be a snare, or a trap. Their false gods had a strong sensual appeal to pleasure and prosperity. Joshua also warned Israel to distrust their own human nature. They must guard their own hearts to keep from following their own lusts. Further, he insisted that Israel should remain faithful to God because God had been faithful to them. Finally, Joshua warned that just as surely as God kept all His promises to bring Israel into the land and subdue their enemies before them, He would also keep His promise to punish Israel if they forsook Him. Israel must be faithful to God, or they would face the discipline of God.

All of this is relevant to the Christian walk with God today. Because Christ died for us, taking upon Himself the wrath of God, we have peace *with* God (Romans 5:1, 9). Our sins have all been paid for, and we are no longer subject to God's judgment. However, we can experience the peace of God only as we live in obedient submission to our Lord (Philippians 4:6–8; Colossians 3:12–17). We are still capable of sinning, and when we sin, we become subject to God's discipline.

Q: Read John 1:12. When a person receives the Lord Jesus as his Savior by believing on His name, what does God give him the right (power) to become?

A: _____

_____

Q: What does Romans 8:1 say about those who are "in Christ Jesus"?

A: _____

_____

Q: Now read Hebrews 12:4–8. While believers who do not "strive against sin" are still called sons and are described as those "whom the Lord loveth" and "whom he receiveth," what are some of the words used in this passage to describe God's response toward sin in one of His sons?

A: _____

_____

God's chastening, or discipline, takes many forms, but its purpose is to get our attention and bring about repentance so we can be restored to fellowship with Him. The discipline of God is rooted in a love so strong that He must chasten those who are His to correct them and draw them back to His side.

Q: What do you believe the Bible teaches God will do to you if you are a believer who willfully disobeys Him?

A: _____

_____

Q: Briefly describe a time when you believe you experienced the chastening of God.

A: _____

_____

Q: How did you respond to it?

A: _____

_____

Some time later Joshua called for a second meeting with the leaders of Israel. A total of about thirty years had passed since Israel crossed Jordan into Canaan, and probably no more than a year or two since the meeting described in Joshua 23. This meeting apparently included a general assembly of Israel besides just the leaders, and at the meeting Joshua delivered what would be his farewell address to the nation. This was not simply Joshua's reminiscences and observations. He specifically states that this is a message from the Lord.

Joshua began by listing several significant events in Israel's history, starting with a fact that must have been pretty embarrassing—their forefathers were idolaters. The Lord wanted Israel to remember that they did not become God's chosen nation because their forefathers were good, but because God is good. Joshua continued to describe how God took Abraham out of Ur and led him to Canaan, how He used Moses and Aaron to redeem Israel from Egypt, how He provided for the Israelites in the wilderness, and how He had brought them into the inheritance He had promised. Throughout, Joshua was emphasizing the fact that everything they were and everything they had were gifts of God's grace. They hadn't earned any of it. All of Israel's history demonstrated two truths: God hates sin, and God calls out and delivers His people. It was God who had brought them to this point, and only He could take them on from here. All of this served to drive home the fact of Israel's dependence upon God.

Joshua then started telling Israel what God expected of them. The most fundamental need for Israel's future was individual, personal devotion to God and rejection of idolatry. They were to serve God "in sincerity and in truth" (Joshua 24:14). Their obedience was not to be occasional or half-hearted, but constant and single-minded.

With the faithfulness and power of God and the worthlessness and impotence of the heathen gods in view, Joshua charged Israel to make up their minds—"choose you this day whom ye will serve" (Joshua 24:15). Not surprisingly, the people answered with a vow never to forsake the Lord to serve other gods. Joshua's reply was probably startling when he told them, "Ye cannot serve the Lord: for he is an holy God; he is a jealous God; he will not forgive your transgressions" (Joshua 24:19). He warned them that God is jealous—He will not tolerate divided loyalty, but would turn and consume them if they forsook Him. When the people responded that they were serious, that they really intended to serve the Lord whole-heartedly, Joshua issued a further warning—"Ye are witnesses against yourselves that ye have chosen you the Lord, to serve him" (24:22). When they responded, "We are witnesses," they meant that they were willing to go on record for this decision. This was not just an emotional response to a popular leader's last plea. It was a purposeful choice to identify with God alone and obey Him fully, and they were willing to be held accountable for it. They had bound themselves by an oath that the Lord would be their God, and they would be His people. Joshua set up a stone as a historical marker to memorialize the event.

Q: If the most fundamental need of Israel's future was for individual, personal devotion to God and rejection of anything that would take the place of God in their lives, what does that say about your own need?

A: _____

_____

This message still applies to each of us today. Our salvation, even our very existence, is a gift from God. We owe Him everything. The Lord Jesus has an absolute right to demand our whole-hearted, single-minded devotion and obedience. The idea that since we are saved we can live like we please goes completely opposite to what the Bible says. What the Bible actually teaches is that since we are saved we can live as He pleases.

Genuine conversion involves a dual response to the gospel: rejecting your own sin and accepting the grace of God. A person who is truly born again, or regenerated, will recognize that his sin is not just harmful, but that it is actually treason against the Sovereign Creator God, and its penalty is death. Fearing the wrath of God that he knows he deserves, he repents, turning from his sin to the Lord Jesus. Repentance involves not only rejecting your sin, but accepting the Lord Jesus Christ as your only hope for rescue. It is impossible to have your sins forgiven without also having a change of loyalty. Even the mature Christian will still struggle with submission, but no one who consciously rejects Christ's authority has truly come to Him.

Q: Have you repented of your sin and turned to Christ?

A: _____

_____

Q: If not, why not?

A: _____

_____

Q: If so, what areas of your life do you know have been less than
fully submitted to Christ's authority?

A: _____

_____

Q: What will you do about those things?

A: _____

_____

Sometimes when believers really want to do something that they
know the Bible says is wrong, they will make the following argument: "God wants me to be happy. Doing this thing He has forbidden will make me happy. Therefore, God really won't mind if I go
ahead and do it anyway." The problem with this whole argument
is in the very first statement. God is not nearly so concerned with
making you happy as with making you holy (1 Peter 1:14–16). The
only thing that will keep you from being caught up in sin through
the temptations of this world and your own lusts is for you to be oc-
cupied with God's Word.

By God's grace, may each of us be able to say at the end of our
lives, "I have fought a good fight, I have finished my course, I have
kept the faith" (2 Timothy 4:7). God expects that of each of us.

Q: Write a brief paragraph describing the kind of man God wants
you to be and what you should do to become The Man You
Could Be.

A: _____

_____

_____

_____

_____

_____

PROJECTS FOR DEVELOPING AN OBEDIENT FAITH

1. Read Ephesians 1:3–14; 3:14–21, and Colossians 1:9–19, then
   list several genuine blessings from God in your life and thank
   Him for His goodness.

   _____

   _____

   _____

   _____

   _____

   _____

   _____

2. At the close of Joshua's farewell address to Israel, the people
   pledged undivided and undying loyalty to God, and Joshua
   erected a simple monument to memorialize the event. It's a
   great concept—marking significant events in our spiritual
   growth. Write brief accounts of at least two or three events in
   your life that have been significant to your spiritual growth.

   _____

   _____

   _____

   _____

   _____

   _____

   _____

   _____

Conclusion

You've finished! If you've worked your way through all the lessons, answered all the questions, and memorized all the verses, you've done a lot. I'm proud of you. I hope you've taken the lessons to heart.

There are several things that I hope you've learned in the process of working through these lessons from the life of Joshua. In general, I hope you've gained a greater appreciation for the practical help you can find through the study of Old Testament history. I also hope that in the process you've improved your knowledge of how to study the Bible. This can help you with your own independent Bible reading and study in the years ahead. More particularly, I hope you've grown in your understanding of Joshua as a great man of God while learning something about his place in Israel's history. He is, truly, an excellent role model for young men today.

Beyond the academic goal of teaching you a little more about the Bible, there have also been several important spiritual lessons for you to have learned through this course. As I've been pointing out along the way, Joshua's life story serves as a sort of metaphor for the believer's life in Christ. Of course the most important goal of this study has been to help you recognize your own personal need of Jesus Christ as your Lord and Savior. Just as Joshua was a slave and had to be rescued by God, you were born in bondage to sin and have to be rescued by Jesus Christ through faith in Him. Knowledge about the Bible is worthless if you don't know Jesus Christ. Have you admitted your own sinfulness? Do you believe that Jesus is the Son of God Whose life, death, and resurrection provide the only payment that will satisfy God's wrath toward your sins? Have you acknowledged Jesus as the rightful ruler of your life Who alone can save you from your sins? Have you asked Him to forgive your sins and take control of your life? Your eternal salvation rests upon faith in Christ alone. The Lord Jesus asked it this way: "For what is a man profited, if he shall gain the whole world, and lose his own soul? or what shall a man give in exchange for his soul?" (Matthew 16:26).

If you've been saved for very long, you know that real Christians still have problems. Like Joshua and Israel, believers today have to deal with tragedy, loss, illness, death, temptation, failure, defeat, discouragement, and all the other difficulties faced by people everywhere. God saves us from the penalty and power of sin, but He does not promise to deliver us from all hardships. When Joshua and Israel entered Canaan, they did not begin a lifelong vacation of rest and relaxation. No, they picked up their swords and fought enemies. In all their fighting, God was helping. God had given them the land, but they had to fight to take it. When they fought their enemies, it was God who gave the victory, often in miraculous ways.

It has been my prayer that this study would help prepare you to survive, even thrive, in the midst of the challenges of life. To do so, you must first of all believe everything God tells you in the Bible, then you must do what God tells you to do, letting God work through you. You cannot get to heaven by trying to obey, but if you are on your way to heaven by faith in Christ, you should do your best to obey. God expects His children to be obedient. That is why I've said so often in this study that victory comes through obedient faith.

It's a little confusing, isn't it: God promises to do things in and through us, then He tells us to do them; and when we do them, He gives us the ability to do things we couldn't have done without Him. It's a kind of teamwork with God as the Commander, Guide, and Power Source, and us as the willing and active tools in His hands. Have you surrendered to your Commander, Guide, and Power Source? Will you let Him use you as a tool in His hands? If so, you can have the strength and wisdom you need to become *The Man You Could Be.*